SARONIC

And Eastern Peloponnese

ROD HEIKELL

Tetra Publications Ltd

Cover photo: Idhra harbour.

Other books by Rod Heikell

Ionian Tetra Publications

Mediterranean France and Corsica Imray, Laurie, Norie & Wilson

Italian Waters Pilot Imray, Laurie, Norie & Wilson

Greek Waters Pilot Imray, Laurie, Norie & Wilson

Turkish Waters Pilot Imray, Laurie, Norie & Wilson

A Pocket Guide to the SE Aegean (with Mike Harper) Imray, Laurie, Norie & Wilson

Mediterranean Sailing A & C Black

Mediterranean Cruising Handbook Imray, Laurie, Norie & Wilson

The Turquoise Coast of Turkey NET Publications

Danube - A River Guide Imray, Laurie, Norie & Wilson

Published by
Tetra Publications Ltd
29 St Cyprians St, London SW17 8SZ, England

Heikell Rod
Saronic
I. Greece. Saronic Yachtsmans Guide
I. Title

ISBN 0-9518691-16

CAUTION
While every care has been taken to ensure accuracy, neither the Publishers nor the Author will hold themselves responsible for errors, omissions or alterations to this publication. They will at all times be grateful to receive information which tends to the improvement of the work.

Printed at the Bath Press, Avon

All the plans in this book were produced by Imray, Laurie, Norie & Wilson.
All the photographs in the book were taken by Rod Heikell unless stated otherwise.

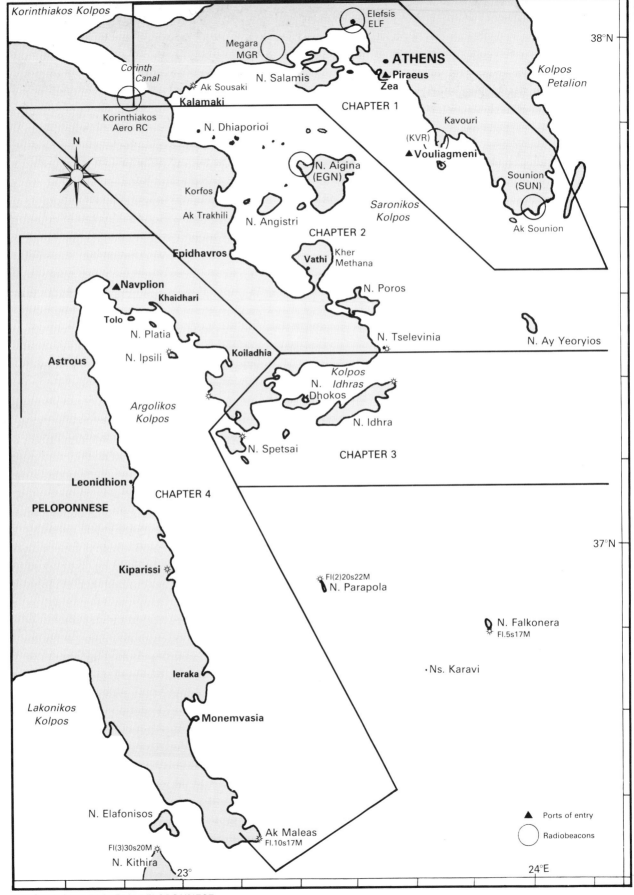

SARONIC AND EASTERN PELOPONNESE

CONTENTS

PREFACE

In the spring of 1978 I set off on my first flotilla from Spetsai with the brochure produced by the company and a couple of charts. I hadn't been to half of the places and my apparent knowledge for the skippers' briefings was derived from deciphering every mark and squiggle on the chart and a large dollop of bull. I soon decided that I'd keep my job and the charterers would be better served if they had plans of the places they were going to and some pilotage notes. The hostess decided the notes should also indicate what facilities there were and what there was of interest to see and do ashore. That first rough guide for the Saronic flotilla in 1978 set in motion a whole series of yachtsman's guides for countries in the Mediterranean and it is ironic that it has now turned full circle and here I am producing a guide to the Saronic again.

There were a number of reasons the area was chosen for flotilla sailing. It has a good mix of quite sophisticated towns and tourist resorts and small villages and anchorages off the tourist track. The wind and weather are benign and consistent with good sailing winds throughout the season and few gales. It has ancient sites close by for history buffs to ponder over. And an almost perpetually blue sky and translucent water. This all remains true of the area and it is as good a sailing area as it ever was - particuarly when the *meltemi* is howling down through the Cyclades to the east.

Inevitably it is popular in the summer and its proximity to Athens means it is within easy reach for weekend excursions. Fortunately most boats from Athens have a magnetic attraction for the main ports of Aegina, Hydra and Spetsai and these are good places to stay away from on busy summer weekends. Little is lost because there are numerous harbours or anchorages nearby and you can nip around to the busy harbours in the morning when everyone has left. I hope this book enables you to navigate your way around the area and persuades you to look at some of the lesser known spots off the better known 'milk run'.

If things have changed in the time between writing and going to print then write to me care of the publishers. To those who helped me put this book together my thanks. I would especially like to thank Willie Wilson of Imray, Laurie, Norie & Wilson for his encouragement and for the production of the plans from my originals; Roy and Barbara Stacey dreaming of boats in land-locked Tooting; Rob and Nell Stuart for digital knowledge; Chris and Luvvy in Poros - thanks for fixing the masthead light on the green teashop; to Sotiros Kouvaras of Greek Sails for dinners and good company; to Julian Blatchley and Nicole for the mini-cruise while waiting (in vain) for the *meltemi* to subside; to Graham and Katrina Sewell of s/y *Songline*, proofer of the Aegean award; to Joe and Robin Charlton for shelter and company; to the large motorboat in Idhra who dropped it's anchor across mine - I told you I'd be able to haul it up in the morning; and to Odile who edited this book and struggled with the layout on the VDU screen, my thanks for the perseverance and long hours you put into it all.

Rod Heikell
London and Homps 1993

Papas. Poros.

Fisherman. Vathi on Methana.

Fisherman. Astrous.

Cafeneion idler. Ermioni.

THE SARONIC

About Greece

History

One of the problems I constantly encounter in Greece is putting historical events into perspective. When did the Venetians colonise the Greek islands? And which islands? When was the classical period in Greek antiquity? Who were the Myceneans? I am not going to elaborate on any of these, but I have assembled the following historical order of things in Greece (with a slight bias to the Saronic) in order to give some perspective to historical events. For detail, wrangling over dates and places, and for explanations of what went on, the reader will have to consult other sources.

Neolithic Period Little is known of early Neolithic life in Greece. Around 6500 BC early stone age settlers crossed the Bosphorus to mainland Europe and probably used primitive boats and rafts to get to islands close to the Asian shore. In the Franchthi Cave in the cliffs near Koilas numerous prehistoric remains have been found including a skeleton from the Mesolithic period that may provide important clues to early Neolithic life in Europe. Around 4000 BC the Cycladic civilisation was well established and from the wide distribution of their distinctive geometric designs we know that there was communication between the islands on a regular basis.

Minoan Period (2000 to 1450? BC) Around 2500 BC new colonists moved down into Greece from the Balkans and Turkey bringing bronze weapons and tools with them. The Minoan civilisation was concentrated on Crete and Thira where the art of pottery and metalwork was brought to a high art. They also seem to have brought the art of

comfortable and civilised living to a high art as well. The Minoans colonised few places and appeared happy to police the seas with their vessels and so procure order and peace while permitting other peoples to go about their business. The civilisation ended abruptly around 1450 BC, probably from one of the biggest eruptions known when Thira exploded and tidal waves estimated to be 70 ft high together with earthquakes and ash destroyed the civilisation overnight.

Mycenean Period (1500 to 1100 BC) With the demise of the Minoans, the Myceneans, a Greek speaking race based at Mycenae in the Argolid, stepped into the power vacuum. These are the Acheaens of Homer and the Trojan War fought around 1200 BC is thought to be a battle brought about by the Myceneans seeking trade outlets in the Black Sea. The centre of power appears to have been at Mycenae on the Plain of Argos and excavations have revealed extensive fortifications, a palace, and the characteristic beehive tombs in one of which Schlieman found what he believed to be the death mask of Agamemnon. The Myceneans were displaced by the Dorians who invaded from the north bringing with them Iron Age technology.

Greek Civilisation (1100 to 200 BC) This title covers a multitude of sins. From around 1100 to 900 BC the Greek 'Dark Age' wiped out not only culture, but also written language. While the Greek speaking Dorians existed in this dark twilight, the Phoenicians from the Levant (Syria? Lebanon?) took control of the sea routes. By 800 BC a written language was emerging and Homer, possibly a native of Khios, penned the *Iliad* and the *Odyssey*.From 750 to 500 BC (the Archaic or Classical period) city-states (*Polis*) sprang up all over Greece, some more powerful than others, some in alliance with others, but all trading with one another and bound together in a loose defence pact. Colonies were established all around the Mediterranean.

The Persian Wars (500 to 478 BC) pulled the city-states together around Athens and cemented the Delian league based around the tiny island of Delos in the Cyclades. The Hellenic period arrived with the final defeat of the Persians and the establishment of Athens as the power base. The Peloponnesian War (431 to 404 BC) between Athens and Sparta divided the islands and the city-states and caused much hardship for inhabitants whose government opted for the wrong side at the wrong time as the war raged back and forth. The war weakened both Athens and Sparta leaving the way open for Phillip II of Macedonia and later his son Alexander the Great to take control of Greece, though little changed under the Greek educated Alexander.

The Romans (200 BC to 295 AD) A weak Greece was easy prey for the Romans and they declared war on Phillip V of Macedonia in 202 BC. Octavius defeated Anthony and Cleopatra at Actium near Preveza and cemented the Roman Empire into a whole after a decade of infighting. Roman rule had little cultural influence on Greece while things Greek, everything from architectural style to cuisine, had a profound effect on the Roman way of life. Greek cities were largely autonomous owing allegiance to Rome and Greek remained the official language. In 295 AD, weakened by attacks from tribes on the edges of the empire and beset by difficulties within, Diocletian split the empire into two.

Byzantium (330 to 1204 AD) The foundation of Constantinople and the rise of Byzantium marks the rise of the first Christian Empire. Byzantine rule of it's empire was constantly beset by invasions from the north and south. The Slavs, Avars, Goths, Huns, Vandals, and Bulgars came down from the north while the Saracens sailed across from the south. The islands were depopulated and towns and villages contracted in size and moved away from a precarious shoreline. At times the Byzantines drove the invaders out, but as Ottoman power grew the empire shrank away from it's island territory in Greece.

The Venetians (1204 to 1550) In 1204 the Fourth Crusade sacked Constantinople (ostensibly their allies!) and parts of the Byzantine Empire were parcelled out to adventurers from the European nobility. The Venetians, who had transported the crusaders, emerged with a large chunk of Byzantine territory as their prize. The sea route down through the Ionian islands and around the Peloponnese into the Aegean was established and though the Venetians secured some parts of the Saronic the area was not critical for their trade routes to the east and was often ignored.

Epidavros theatre.

The Turks (1460 to 1830) In 1453 the Ottoman Turks took Constantinople and ended the rule of Byzantium. By the end of the 16th century most of Greece was under Turkish control. Around the Peloponnese and the Aegean islands the Venetians continued to battle the Turks for territory though it was a losing battle against the omnipotent Turk.

The War of Independence (1822 to 1830) In 1821 the Greek flag was raised at Kalavrita The Peloponnese. In 1822 the Turks massacred 25,000 people on the island of Khios and so aroused Greek passions that many took up arms against the Turks. Spetsai and Idra were amongst the first islands to commit there hitherto commercial fleets to the war effort and harried the Turks in the Saronic and Argolic gulfs, scoring some notable successes with their use of fire-ships. The war was effectively won when a combined English, French, and Russian fleet destroyed the larger Turkish and Egyptian fleet at Navarino. The provisional capital of newly liberated Greece was at Aegina until it was moved to Navplion in 1828. Athens was made the capital in 1834.

Modern Greece The newly born republic got off to a shaky start and after a series of assassinations the western powers put a Bavarian prince on the throne. He proved an insensitive and unpopular ruler and was deposed by a popular revolt in 1862. In 1863 a new ruler, George I from Denmark, was chosen and the British relinquished control of the Ionian islands to encourage support. The boundaries of Greece expanded with the acquisition of Thessaly and the Epirus in 1881 and Macedonia and the northern Aegean islands in the Balkan wars (1912-13).

The Greeks fought on the Allied side in the First World War and with the defeat of the Turks on the Axis side, embarked on a disastrous campaign to acquire territory in Asia Minor. When the Greeks were finally driven out the Turkish population remaining in Greece was exchanged for Greeks in Turkey. Greece fought in the Second World War on the side of the Allies and obtained the last of her territory, the Dodecanese, from the Italians at the end of the war. Civil war split the country until 1947 when a Conservative government was elected. In 1967 the army took power with the notorious junta of the Colonels which ushered in seven years of autocratic and harsh rule. Democracy returned in 1974 with Karamanlis. The first Socialist government, *PASOK*, under Papandreou, was elected in 1981. In 1986 Greece joined the European Community. In 1990 the conservative *Nea Democratia* party was elected.

The Battle of Salamis

The survival of Greece as Greece and of Athens as the centre of Greek civilisation hinged on this sea battle in the narrow channel at the eastern end of Salamis. Today as you survey the topography of the place it is difficult to reconcile what you see with the events. Industrial and naval installations cover the land to make it one of the least evocative sights around. Yet the geography of the place remains the same despite some scholarly wrangling over what was where and the fact that the land has sunk some two metres since the Greeks and the Persians fought it out here.

By 480 BC Xerxes had conquered a large part of Greece. From Persia he easily subdued the Greek colonies on the coast of Asia Minor and marched his army up the coast and across the Dardanelles on a floating bridge made up of his naval fleet. The vast army and the fleet crossed northern Greece and then headed south to take Athens. At this stage all that opposed his total conquest of Greece was the Greek fleet at Salamis and the Spartans on the Peloponnese.

Before the Persians had arrived at Athens most of the population had been evacuated, many of them to nearby Troezen as the discovery of the Troezen stone detailing Themistokles evacuation plans now makes apparent. The remainder of the population was assembled at Salamis and when the Persians arrived at Athens there was some panic to get them away. After evacuating the last of the population Themistokles persuaded the assorted admirals to stay in the narrows under the island and engage the Persian fleet there. This was not easy for him to do. The Spartans wanted to retire to the isthmus at Corinth where most of their army was assembled. Others wanted to retire to the Peloponnese and take on the Persians there. Themistokles pointed out that if they did not engage the Persian fleet at Salamis then the islands of Aegina and Poros and the city states on the eastern Peloponnese would be easy prey for the Persians. Agreement was somehow reached and Themistokles put his cunning plan into action.

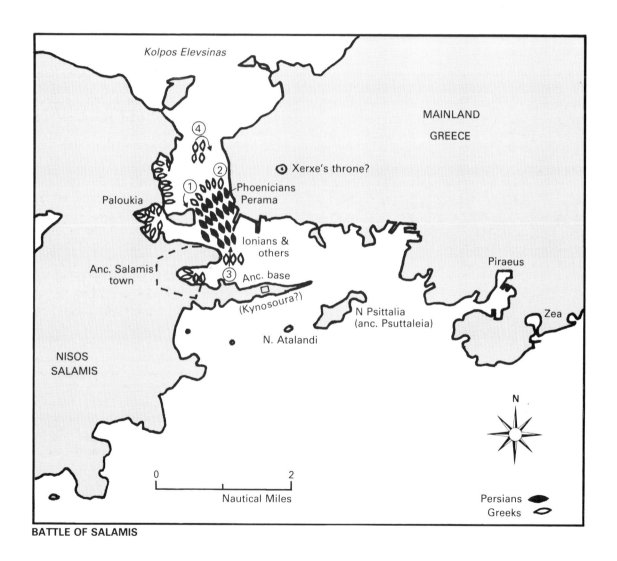

BATTLE OF SALAMIS

At this point sometime in September 480 BC the Persian fleet was assembled in Faliron and the Greek fleet in the narrows at Salamis. The Persian fleet far outnumbered the Greek fleet, though the Persians did not have anything like the thousand ships the Greeks later credited them with. On the open water the Persians would certainly have defeated the Greeks. Xerxes army could then have mopped up the remnants of the combined Greek army. The Persian generals and admirals advised on different strategies with some wanting to sail to the Peloponnese and others wanting to starve the Greeks out of Salamis. Then Themistokles sent his false message.

Xerxes had numerous spies in the Greek camp and via one of them Themistokles leaked a message that the Greeks were squabbling amongst themselves (which in fact they were) and that if the Persian fleet attacked then certain of the Greek factions would come over to the Persian side. Ignoring the advice of his admirals Xerxes ordered the fleet to sea to attack the Greeks at Salamis. The Egyptian squadron of around 200 ships was dispatched to guard the western entrance and stop the Greeks escaping that way. The remainder of the fleet rowed into the narrows on the east side of Salamis.

The number of Greek ships is variously numbered at 310 (Aeschylus) or 380 (Herodotus). Most of these were smaller and more manoeuvrable than the ships of the Persian fleet. The best of Xerxes fleet, the Phoenicians, squeezed through the narrows and then attempted to fan out into battle formation. At this point the Greek fleet emerged from behind the small island in the narrows and caught the Phoenicians in disarray. Aeschylus tells us that the first ship rammed was hit on the stern and must therefore have been turning. The crippled ships in front were prevented from retiring by the ships coming up behind and the Persian fleet was soon jammed in a hopeless muddle in the narrows. The Greek ships picked off those ships penetrating through the crippled ships in the front. Such was the confusion that the Persians rammed their own ships -

An exact replica of a trireme designed in England and constructed in Greece.

Herodotus tells us that Artemisia, queen of Halicarnassos and the Carians, rammed and sank one of her own ships in the chaos.

There are some elements of the accounts which are difficult to piece together. The Corinthian fleet apparently headed north away from the battle only to turn abruptly and row back into the melee. Herodotus tells us that the Corinthian fleet was distinguished in battle so it has been assumed that the retreat by the Corinthian ships was a feint designed to entice the Persian fleet into the narrows when they saw Greek ships apparently fleeing. Aeschylus in his dramatic rendering of the battle gives much prominence to the capture of the island of Psittalaia by the Greek army after the sea battle. Commentators suggest this was because Aeschylus had been with the Greek land force and wanted them to have a little bit of glory after the brilliant triumph of the navy.

Xerxes had a silver throne set upon the heights over the narrows to watch what he thought was going to be his great victory over the Greeks. Instead he saw his best ships destroyed and within a few days he returned to Persia. The remainder of his fleet returned to

Asia Minor and was destroyed the next year. This marked the end of Persian designs on Greece and indeed the decline of the Persian empire.

The battle ranks as one of those decisive battles of the world that turned history around. Without the strategy of Themistokles there might have been no continuation of the Greek civilisation that evolved in the centuries after the battle and all it bestowed upon us for better or worse. Salamis did not acquire the legend of Marathon but it was in every way a more significant event.

Language

It should be remembered that the Greek spoken today, demotic Greek, is not ancient Greek though it is largely derived from it. Anyone who speaks ancient Greek will be able to pick up a little over 50 per cent of the Greek spoken today, though the pronunciation may not be what you expect. In rendering Greek from the Greek alphabet into the Roman alphabet there are very real difficulties and there are no absolutes, just guidelines.

Greek is difficult to master because right from the start you come up against the Greek alphabet which for most people may as well be hieroglyphics. Yet the alphabet can be conquered with a little persistence and common words and phrases to get you by in the tavernas and bars and on the street can be picked up by ear. One of the obstacles to learning Greek is that you so often come across someone speaking English that the need to learn Greek evaporates. However if you can only learn a few phrases, a `hello' and `good-bye' and `how are you', the effort will be repaid especially in out of the way places. In Appendix I the Greek alphabet and a few useful phrases will be found.

The Greek Orthodox Church

For someone from the west, from the world of Roman Catholicism and Protestantism, the churches and the black robed priests of the Greek Orthodox church constitute another religious world, and so it is. Up until the last meeting of the Council of Nicaea in 787, the western and eastern branches of the church had stumbled along together, growing apart but outwardly united. Post Nicaea the churches grew apart, partly on doctrinal issues, but mostly one suspects because of the geographical and cultural isolation between Rome and Constantinople. In Rome they spoke mostly Latin, in Constantinople Greek. In the west priests were celibate, in the east they married. In Rome the Pope was infallible, in Constantinople articles of faith were decided by a council of bishops. In the west the spirit of God came from the Father and the Son, in the east from the Father.

The overthrow of Constantinople by the Turks in 1453 scattered the church as far afield as Russia and today the Orthodox church is still spread widely across the Balkans and into the steppes. The church was allowed to continue under the Turks and it became a focus for rebellion against the occupiers of Greece.

Today the church, although much weakened in this secular age, still permeates Greek life. For the Greeks the big event of the year is not Christmas, but Easter, *Pasca*. The date of Easter is reckoned in a different way to that in the west, and the celebration is focused on the Resurrection rather than the Crucifixion. On Good Friday a service marks the Descent from the Cross and the *Epitafion* containing the body of Christ is paraded through the streets. In some places an effigy of Judas Iscariot is burnt or blown up. This latter can be a spectacular event as all Greek men love playing with dynamite and the effigy is inevitably stuffed with it. All Greek homes brew up a soup from the offal of the lamb which is to be eaten on the Resurrection and depending on your inclination, the soup may be your sort of dish or you may have problems sampling even a spoonful of assorted tripe and other organs.

Late Saturday night there is the *Anestisi* mass to celebrate Christ's return. In the church all the lights are turned out and then from behind the altar screen the priest appears with a lighted candle and proceeds to light the candles of those in the church. Everyone responds with *Kristos Anesti* (Christ is risen) and there is a procession with the lighted candles through the streets to the sound of fire-crackers and sky-rockets, or any other explosive devices that are to hand. This is not a good time to be in trouble at sea as a lot of out-of-date flares are used up - though don't be tempted yourself as it is against the law to do so and there have been prosecutions. The traditional greeting everyone utters at this time is *Kronia Polla* (Many years or Long life). In the home boiled eggs, traditionally dyed red, are dished out and the normal sport is to bet your egg against the others, in the manner of conkers, or to surprise your friends with a solid rap on the head with the egg to crack the shell.

There are many local saints days in the villages and towns and the whole place will often close down for them even if they are not on the list of state holidays. Greeks normally celebrate not their birthday, but the day of the saint they are named after - their name-day. In some churches there are icons to a saint reckoned to provide an above average service and these will have numerous votive offerings. Many of these are simple affairs, a pressed metal disc showing what blessing is required, whether for an afflicted limb, safety at sea, a new-born baby or a family house. Some of the older votive offerings are more ornate and elaborate, sometimes a painting or a model of a ship where thanks are given for survival at sea, or a valuable brooch or piece of jewellery for some other blessing.

Greek churches are wonderful places, the iconostasis always elaborate and adorned, and the interior a dark and mystical place. It constantly amazes me that even in the most out-of-the-way places, on a rocky islet or a remote headland, that every church and chapel and shrine will be newly white-washed and cleaned and will have an oil lamp burning or ready to burn in it.

Bell tower. Spetsai.

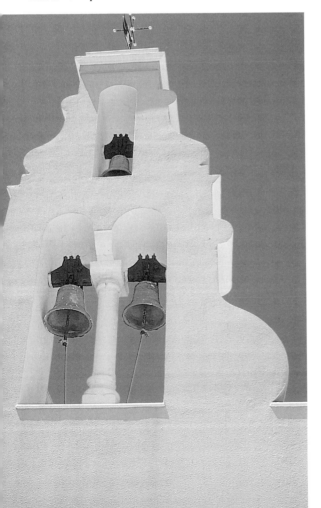

Food

Greek food is not for the gourmet, rather it is plain wholesome cooking that goes with the climate and the Greek idea that a meal is as much a social occasion as a culinary experience. This is not, emphatically not, to say that Greek food is not enjoyable. I love the unadulterated flavours of charcoal grilled fish with a squeeze of lemon over it, or a *salata horiatiki*, the ubiquitous mixed salad swimming in olive oil and peppered with *feta* and black olives - the simplicity of the combination of ingredients brings out the best in them. In some restaurants and in Greek family cooking you

Food with a view

will come across dishes that have been lost in the tourist areas where either the lethargy of taverna owners or the whinging of visitors for a bland 'international' cuisine revolving around steak and chips has removed them from the menu. Some of the island tavernas still have a dish or two specific to the island or region such as Fish Spetsiosa on Spetsai, but for the majority the dishes on the menu are those which are simply prepared and cooked and a few favourites such as *moussaka* and *stifadho*.

The principal meal in Greece is the midday meal and most oven-cooked dishes are prepared in the morning for this meal. In the evening these dishes will simply be partially re-heated and served up as an over-cooked luke-warm mess. Restaurants in Greece are categorised as either an *Estiatorio* (a restaurant), a *Taverna* (a simple tavern), or a *Psistaria* (a restaurant specialising in fresh prepared food, mostly grilled meat), but the distinctions between these have now become so blurred that most restaurants call themselves a taverna.

The menu in a taverna will have two sets of prices, one with service and one without, and since all food comes with service you pay the higher price. In fact waiters are paid on results and the difference between the two prices goes to them which explains why some waiters work their butts off and others, often family who are not paid on results, loaf about ignoring your frantic pleas for a drink. In most Greek tavernas you will be invited into the kitchen or to a counter displaying the food to make your choice, a handy convention that gets over the problem of knowing what it is you are ordering from the menu. Only in the flasher restaurants will you be requested to order from the menu and there will normally be an English translation on the menu or on a board on the wall to help you out.

A typical Greek meal will be a starter and main course with other side dishes ordered at random. Dessert is not normally served in a taverna although you may get fresh fruit or yoghurt. When ordering don't order everything at the same time as it will all arrive at once or sometimes you will get the main course first and the starter second. Often the food will be just warm, it having been set aside to cool as Greeks believe hot food is bad for you, a belief that has some backing from the medical community. If you get everything in order and hot, and things have improved in recent years, you are on a winner. If you don't, just order another bottle of wine and settle yourself in for the evening like the other Greeks around you - after all what have you got to do that's so important after dinner.

Below there is a list of the common dishes you will come across though obviously they vary in finesse and taste from taverna to taverna according to the skills of the cook.

Soups, salads and starters

Avgolemono	Egg and lemon soup, often with a chicken and rice broth.
Fakes	Lentil soup.
Fasolada	Bean soup.
Hortosoupa	Vegetable soup.
Psarossoupa	Fish soup.
Tzatziki	Yoghurt and chopped cucumber dip.
Taramasalata	Fish roe dip.
Melitzanasalata	Aubergine dip.
Patatasalata	Potato salad.
Skordhalia	Potato and garlic dip, sometimes accompanies other dishes as a piquant sauce.
Salata horiatiki	Mixed salad, usually tomatoes, cucumber, onion, green pepper, black olives, and feta.
Domatasalata	Tomato salad.
Salata marouli	Green salad, usually lettuce.
Horta	Spring greens, often including rocket and spinach.
Rizospanaki	Rice mixed with spinach.
Piperies psites	Baked peppers.
Melitzanes tiganites	Fried aubergines, delicious if freshly fried.
Kolokithakia tiganites	Fried courgettes.
Fasolia yigandes plaki	Giant or butter beans in a tomato sauce.
Tiropita	Cheese wrapped in filo pastry, mini-versions of the large snack tiropitas.

Some of the above can accompany the main course.

Main courses

Brizola khirino	Pork chop, normally charcoal grilled.
Brizola mouskhari	Beef chop, normally charcoal grilled.
Paidhakia	Lamb chop, normally charcoal grilled.
Souvlaki	Kebab, usually lamb or beef.
Keftedhes	Meatballs in a sauce, usually tomato but may be an egg and lemon sauce.
Bifteki	A burger, but usually home-made.
Kotopoulo	Chicken, may be oven roasted or spit-roasted.
Kokoretsi	An offal (liver, kidneys, heart, tripe) kebab charcoal grilled. Can be excellent.
Moussaka	Aubergine and mince with a bechamel sauce not unlike a Greek version of shepherds pie.
Stifadho	A meat (usually lamb) and tomato stew.
Pastitsio	Pasta with a mince and cheese sauce, baked in the oven.
Makaronia	Spaghetti, may be with a meat or tomato sauce.
Domates yemistes	Stuffed tomatoes.
Piperies yemiste	Stuffed peppers.
Kolokithia yemiste	Stuffed courgettes.
Melitzanesi imam bayedi	Aubergines baked with tomatoes - a dish

left over from the Turkish occupation that literally means: 'the imam fainted'.

Fish and seafood

Ohtapodhi	Octopus, may be charcoal grilled or cooked in a wine or ink sauce.
Kalamaria	Squid, normally coated in a light batter and deep fried.
Soupia	Cuttle-fish, normally deep fried.
Psaria	Fish, normally fried or grilled.
Barbouni	Red mullet.
Fangri	Bream.
Sfiritha	Grouper.
Tonnos	Tuna.
Xsifia	Swordfish.
Marithes	White Bait normally deep fried, you eat them head and all.
Garidhes	Prawns, normally fried or grilled.
Astakos	Crayfish.

Desserts

Normally desserts and sticky sweets are found in a *Zakhoroplasteia* (patisserie) and in some of the up-market cafes.

Baklava	Honey and nut mixture in filo pastry.
Kataifi	Honey and nut mixture in a sort of shredded wheat.
Rizogalo	Rice pudding.
Galaktobouriko	Custard pie.
Loukoumadhes	Small doughnuts in honey.
Pagota	Ice cream.

There will also be assorted sticky cakes though I personally find most of them too sugary.

Wine

Greek wine is a source of mystery to most western enophiles. There are grape varieties in Greece few have ever encountered before. The production is so inconsistent that wines vary radically from year to year. Most of the wines are oxidised or maderized. Storing wine properly is virtually unknown and most wine is new wine. Until 1969 there was no real government control of wines of a specific origin. To compound all of this wine will often be sitting in a shop window where it gets a dose

Grilled octopus at Aegina. Preferably washed down with *ouzo*, but beer will do.

of sunlight every day. Given all these problems it is amazing that some Greek wine is as good as it is. On the plus side Greek enology is slowly on the mend and given the climatic conditions, the interesting grape varieties, and the excellent results of a few wine producers who have imported new wine-making technology and nurtured their product, the portent for the future is good. We may well see a renaissance in Greek enology that will return it to its ancient elevated status.

Vines for wine-making were growing in Greece before anyone in France or Spain had ever seen or heard of the plant or its product. Estimates vary, but probably sometime around the 13th to the 12th centuries BC Greek viticulture was well established.

The mythic origins of the introduction of the vine are associated with Dionysus and trace the route of the vine from India and/or Asia to Greece. Dionysus was said to be the son of Zeus and Semele (daughter of Cadmus, King of Thebes) who was brought up in India by the nymphs and taught the lore of the vine and wine-making by Silenus and the satyrs - sounds a wonderful childhood to me. He journeyed from India across Asia Minor to Greece bringing the vine and accompanied by a band of followers.

One can imagine a religious cult growing up around wine, the visions and hallucinations from imbibing it could only have been super-natural, and the introduction of it to Greece would have been unstoppable, hence its incorporation into the mythic universe of the ancients. The Homeric *Hymn to Dionysus* tells of his journey around the islands distributing the vine and describes vine leaves sprouting from the masthead of his ship. Nor is it surprising that the cult of Dionysus was associated with the release of mass emotion, was a fertility cult, and that the Dionysian Festival included wild uninhibited dancing and at times violence and sacrifice - all things associated in one way or another with alcohol today.

There is no way we can know what ancient wine was like. It was referred to by its place of origin, thus Pramnian, Maronean, Khian, Thasian, and Koan wine were mentioned by name much as we mention a Bordeaux or Côte du Rhône today. Whether or not it was all resinated as in the ubiquitous *retsina* surviving today is unknown. Most likely amphoras of wine were sealed with a resin mixture to prevent oxidation and this imparted a flavour to the wine. Over time it was assumed that the resin itself, and not the exclusion of oxygen, prevented wine going off and oxidising and so resin was added directly to the wine to produce *retsina*. It is unfortunate that many people only get to drink bottled *retsina* today as the stuff from the barrel is superior and should be drunk as a new wine. Much of the bottled *retsina* and some of the barrel *retsina* is simply bad wine that can only be made to taste palatable by resinating it.

Of the general wines on the market, many are made by co-operatives and the preparation, production, storage and bottling is at best sloppy. Some of the better wines to look out for are:

Agioritikos	From Mt Athos. The red (Cabernet sauvignon) and white (Sauvignon blanc) are good value.
Domaine Carras (*Côtes de .Meliton*)	Good young reds and whites
Naoussa	Good reds.
Lion de Nemea	Good red (Agiorgitiko).
LemnosAO	Good whites.
Paros AO	Whites and reds, though not always consistent.
Santorini AO	Good whites though variable.

There are also a number of Muscats that are considered to be good quality though they are not to my taste. The *Samos Muscat* from the island of the same name is considered the best although *Muscat of Cephalonia* and *Muscat of Patras* produced by *Achaia Clauss* also gets a mention. Sweet red liqueur wine vaguely resembling port is produced from the mavro-daphne grape and *Mavrodaphne of Patras* produced by *Achaia Clauss* and *Mavrodaphne of Cephalonia* are passable port-type wines. Many of the local wine shops have a local Mavrodaphne in stock and this is often acceptable.

In the Saronic and eastern Peloponnese there are a number of wines that deserve mention, though they are not all easily obtainable.

Attica

Most wine production in Attica is of *retsina*, but a few non-resinated wines deserve mention. The grape variety that predominates is the white *savatiano* used for *retsina*.

Boutari Chateau Matsa. Dry white.

Marko Chateau Marko. Dry white.

Cambas Kantza which has an appellation of origin.

Cava Cambas is aged in the bottle for a few years. Dry white.

Peloponnese

Nemea Some excellent full bodied reds produced from the *ayiorytiko* (St Georges) grape which is grown almost exclusively in the Nemea area in an area north of the Argolic Gulf. Appellation of origin sold under the Co-operative's own label *Nemea* are widely available.

Grand Palais Excellent dark reds from the Nemea area but difficult to find.

Cambas Mantinia Dry aromatic white from *moskhofilero* and *asproudes* grown in the Mantinia area around Tripolis.

Retsina

Much of the ubiquitous *retsina* found throughout Greece is made from the *savatiano* grape grown in Attica and brewed and bottled there for the mass market. As I have indicated the bottled variety is best avoided and *retsina* should be drunk fresh from the barrel. *Retsina* should really be drunk with *mezes* and not with a full blown meal but in practice you drink it with whatever you want.

Although *retsina* is traditionally identified with Attica and the *savatiano* grape, in fact it is made all over Greece from a variety of grapes. In Poros, George of the *Drougas,* is something of an authority on *retsina* and when he produces his own is rumoured to take his bed down into the cellar so he can be closer to his 'baby'. Normally the grapes are gathered in September and after mashing go straight into the barrels with the must and the pine resin. Around two kilograms of resin goes into a 1000 litre barrel and George collects his own resin locally. The wine ferments for around forty days before fermentation is stopped. Most of the barrels are old, around forty to fifty years old in George's case, and if a barrel should give bad wine it is immediately burnt. The *retsina* should always be drunk as a new wine within a year. Occasionally red *retsina* is made and George reckons he has produced acceptable resinated reds, but it is not common.

Mikhali's taverna. Leonidhion

BACKGROUND BASICS

Getting There

Anyone coming to the Saronic and Peloponnese will almost inevitably arrive at Athens.

By Air
The main international airport for Greece is at Athens and scheduled and charter flights from around the world land here. Foreign airlines arrive at the east terminal and Olympic flights (both international and internal) arrive at the west terminal. Most people arriving in Athens will come by air and then proceed on to other destinations.

By Taxi
This is far and away the easiest way to get to one of the marinas along the Attic coast or to a ferry or hydrofoil to connect with the islands and Peloponnese further west and south. Like taxi drivers everywhere those serving the airport occasionally dupe visitors into paying rather more than is due, but this is now less true than it used to be and most will ask you for whatever the meter says. As long as the meter is turned on getting around by taxi is quite reasonable.

By Bus
A yellow express bus runs from the airport to Piraeus and another to Syntagma approximately every half hour. A blue bus 101 runs to Piraeus. Every half hour an Olympic Airways shuttle bus runs to the west terminal where you can get buses running along the coast road - blue buses 107 and 109 run from the airport to Piraeus along the coast road stopping near the main marinas.

By Sea
Few ferries connect to Piraeus from other countries and those that do are more like cruise ships than ferries proper. P&O operate a luxury ferry service from Venice to Piraeus and there are a few connections with Cyprus and the Levant, but the latter often change their schedules and frequency.

By Land
It is a long haul down to Greece from northern Europe. From Calais you can get to Ancona in 15 hours if you push it though a couple of days is more relaxed. From Ancona and Brindisi there are ferries to Corfu, Igoumenitsa and Patras. It is also possible to drive down through Germany, Austria, and the former Yugoslavia to northern Greece and then across Greece to the Ionian, but this is something of a marathon taking at least two to three days hard driving and the trip through former Yugoslavia has nothing to recommend it. Until the Serbs, Croats and Muslims sort themselves out the trip through the civil war zone is at present hazardous to say the least and the area should be considered a no-drive zone. You can keep a car in Greece for six months renewable for another six months if you take it out and bring it in again - after that you will have to pay duty on it, EC regulations notwithstanding.

Getting Around

Ferries
Passenger and car ferries all leave from Piraeus with few exceptions. Passenger ferries operate on a regular basis to Aegina, Anghistri, Methana, Poros, Ermioni, Idhra, Spetsai, Kiparissi and Monemvasia. Obviously there are more frequent services to the more popular island destinations like Aegina, Poros, Idhra and Spetsai than to lesser known spots like Anghistri or Kiparissi. On the Aegina-Methana-Poros run a semi-planing fast ferry service also operates.

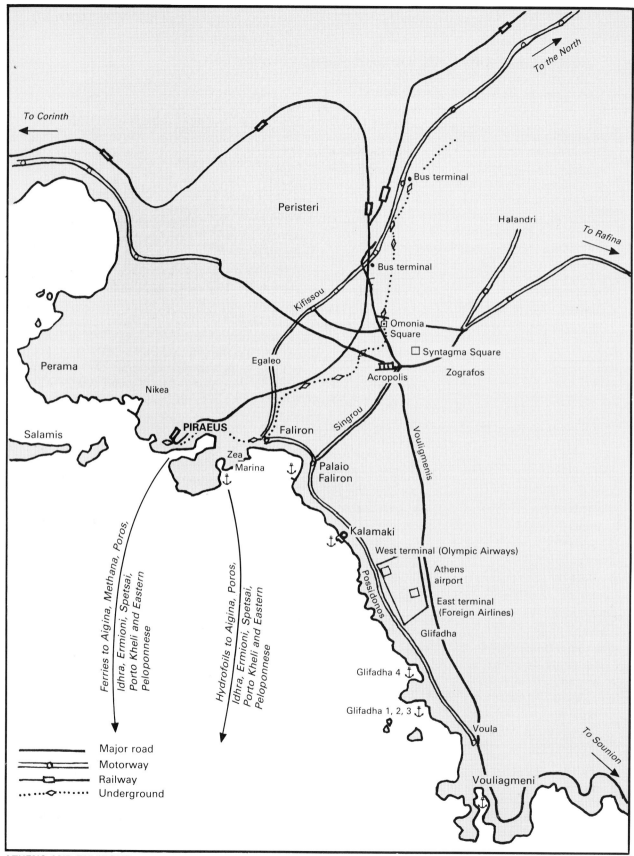

To Corinth

Peristeri

Bus terminal

Halandri

To Rafina

Kifissou

Bus terminal

Omonia
Square

Syntagma Square

Egaleo

Acropolis

Zografos

Perama

Nikea

Singrou

Vouligmenis

PIRAEUS

Faliron

Salamis

Zea
Marina

Palaio
Faliron

Kalamaki

West terminal (Olympic Airways)

Athens
airport

East terminal
(Foreign Airlines)

Possidonos

Glifadha

Ferries to Aigina, Methana, Poros,
Idhra, Ermioni, Spetsai,
Porto Kheli and Eastern
Peloponnese

Hydrofoils to Aigina, Poros,
Idhra, Ermioni, Spetsai,
Porto Kheli and Eastern
Peloponnese

Glifadha 4

Glifadha 1, 2, 3

Voula

To Sounion

Major road

Motorway

Railway

Underground

Vouliagmeni

ATHENS AND ENVIRONS

Landing-barge type ferries that take cars really only operate to Aegina on a frequent service with some going on to Methana and Poros. They take foot passengers as well.

Hydrofoils

An extensive hydrofoil system connects most of the islands and main ports on the Peloponnese in this area and this is one of the best ways to get around. Most of the hydrofoils on the Flying Dolphin service leave from Zea except for services to Aegina which run from Piraeus. The hydrofoils are fast (32 or 36 knots), punctual, clean, and often fully booked in the height of summer on national holidays. They may vibrate a lot and are noisy but they run in nearly all weather. Most of the time you can book a seat half and hour before departure at the office near the hydrofoil berth at Zea. Otherwise there is an office beside Platia Freatidis on the main road near Zea.

Regular services run throughout the day to Aegina, Methana, Poros, Idhra, Ermioni, Porto Kheli, and Spetsai. There are a number of express services which do not stop at every port. Less regular services run to Leonidhion, Tiros, Kiparissi, Ieraka, Monemvasia and into the Argolic Gulf to Tolon, Astrous and Navplion.

Fast Catamaran

Recently a fast (38 knots) catamaran service has been introduced running from Piraeus to Poros, Idhra and Porto Kheli. Like the hydrofoils the service is punctual and the ferry modern and well equipped and even faster than the hydrofoils.

Water-Taxis and Tripper Boats

In the more touristy areas like Idhra and Spetsai water-taxis run trips to nearby beaches or villages. Tripper boats also run from anywhere there is a sizeable concentration of tourists and it is possible to get a one-way trip on one of these.

Buses

Local bus services vary widely on the islands and Peloponnese, but even the best of the services are infrequent. To get about by bus

Supercat ferry at Porto Kheli. It runs a regular service from Piraeus down through the islands to Porto Kheli at around 38 knots.

you will need to check departure times the day before and to exercise a little and sometimes a lot of patience. Between the larger towns and resorts on the Peloponnese there are more frequent services, but the best of these can still only be described as intermittent and you will have to budget to spend fairly large chunks of time if you are going to get around this way.

Taxis

Most of the islands and the mainland towns and larger villages have taxis or can phone for one. Fares are reasonable as long as there is a meter and it works, or the price is roughly agreed upon first. In some of the more touristy spots tourists are fleeced by drivers, but on the whole little of this goes on.

Hire Cars and Bikes

In many of the tourist resorts you can hire a car or jeep, or more commonly a motor-bike of some description. Hire cars and jeeps are expensive in Greece and if there are not four people it is not really worth it unless you are feeling frivolous.

Hire motor-bikes come in all shapes and sizes from battered Honda 50's to 500cc brutes. It is rare to be asked for a license, but the operator will normally hold your passport. It is also rare to be offered a helmet. The reliability of hire bikes varies considerably with some bikes only a year or so old and others still struggling along after years of battering by would-be TT riders. On the whole I have found the Honda/Suzuki/ Yamaha step-through 50's to be the most reliable even when getting on in years and the larger tyres compared to scooters like *Vespas* make them safer on gravel roads.

All of the operators charge you for insurance, but read the small print as it doesn't seem to cover you for very much. You are expected to return the bike if it breaks down and to pay for any damage to the bike if you have an accident. Bear in mind that Greece has the highest accident rate in Europe after Portugal and that on a bike you are vulnerable to injury. Even coming off on a gravel road at relatively low speed can cause serious gravel burns, so despite the heat it is best to wear long trousers and solid footwear. Roads on the islands are usually tarmac for the major routes and gravel for the others. Despite all these warnings a hire bike is the best way to get inland and with care you can see all sorts of places it would be difficult for a car to get to.

Motorbikes of one description or another can be hired in most tourist spots and are the cheapest way of getting around inland, but keep your wits about you when dealing with local traffic. Greece has the worst record in the EC for traffic accidents.

Walking

There are some fine walks around the islands and on the Peloponnese coast. The main problem is finding a good map as most locally produced maps should be treated with a healthy scepticism. Tracks which have long since disappeared will be shown and new tracks will be omitted. The best policy is to set out with the spirit of exploration uppermost and not plan to necessarily arrive somewhere, rather to dawdle along the away. This mode of walking is encouraged by the energy-sapping heat of the summer. Take stout footwear, a good sun-hat, sunglasses, sun-bloc cream, and most importantly a bottle of water.

Shopping and Other Facilities

Provisioning

In all but the smallest village you will find you can obtain basic provisions and in the larger villages and tourist areas there will be a variety of shops catering for your needs. Greece now has a lot more imported goods from the other EC countries and you will be able to find familiar items, peanut butter, bacon, breakfast cereals, even baked beans in the larger super-markets and specialist shops. Imported items are of course more expensive than locally produced goods. Shopping hours are roughly 0800 to 1300 and 1630 to 2000, though shops will often remain open for longer hours in the summer if there are customers around, especially in tourist spots.

Meat Is usually not hung for long and is butchered in a peculiarly eastern Mediterranean way - if you ask for a chicken to be quartered the butcher picks up his cleaver and neatly chops the chicken into four lumps. Salami and bacon are widely available in mini-markets.

Fish Except for smaller fish is generally expensive. Some fish like red snapper and grouper are very expensive and prawns and crayfish have a hefty price tag except off the beaten track.

Fruit and vegetables Fresh produce used to be seasonal, but now EC imports mean more is available longer. It is prudent to wash fruit and vegetables before eating them raw.

Bread Greek bread straight out of the oven is delicious, but it doesn't keep well. Small milk loaves called tspureki keep longer than the normal bread and in some places brown or rye bread can be found and this also keeps better than your average white loaf.

Staples Many items are often sold loose. Some staples, loose or packaged, may have weevils.

Cheese Imported cheeses such as Dutch *edam* or *gruyère* are now widely available courtesy of the EC. Local hard cheeses can also be found and *feta* is available everywhere.

Yoghurt Greek yoghurt is the best in the world as far as I am concerned. Use it instead of salad dressing or cream.

Canned goods Local canned goods are good and cheap, particularly canned fruit. Canned meat is usually imported and expensive.

Coffee and tea Instant coffee is comparatively expensive. Local coffee is ground very fine for 'Greek coffee' and tends to clog filters. Imported ground coffee is available.

Wines, beer and spirits Bottled wine varies from good to terrible and is not consistent, usually because it is not stored properly. Wine can be bought direct from the barrel in larger villages and towns and at least you get to taste before you buy. *Retsina* is also available bottled or from the barrel. Beer is brewed under license (*Amstel* and *Henninger* are the most common), is a light lager type and eminently palatable. Local spirits, *ouzo* not dissimilar to *pastis*, and Greek brandy often referred to by the most common brand name as just *Metaxa*, are good value and can be bought bottled or from the barrel.

Banks

Eurocheques, postcheques, travellers cheques, the major credit cards (*Access and Visa*) and charge cards (*American Express* and *Diners Club*) are accepted in the larger towns and tourist resorts. You will need your passport for identification. For smaller places carry cash. Banks are open from 0800 - 1300 Monday to Friday. Most post offices and some travel agents will change travellers cheques and Eurocheques.

Post

Post offices can be found in larger villages and towns. Mail can be sent to them c/o Poste Restante and the service is reliable. One tip: get the assistant to look under your first name, Esq., and the boats name as well as your surname. You will need your passport for identification.

Telephones

You can direct dial from almost anywhere in Greece. The telephone system is not too bad although it is not unusual to get a crackly line and sometimes to be cut off or find someone else talking on your line. Telephone calls can be made from a kiosk with an orange top to it, a blue top kiosk is for domestic calls only. In the towns there will be an OTE (Overseas Telephone Exchange) where you can make a metered call and pay the clerk on completion. Telephone calls can also be made from metered telephones in a *periptero* although the charge will be higher than at the OTE

Public Holidays

Jan 1	New Years Day
Jan 6	Epiphany
Mar 25	Independence Day
May 1	May Day
Aug 15	Assumption
Oct 28	*Ochi* ('No') Day
Dec 25	Christmas Day
Dec 26	St Stephens Day
Movable	
First Day of Lent	
Good Friday	
Easter Monday	
Ascension	

In addition many of the islands or regions have local Saints days when a holiday may be declared and some shops and offices will close.

SAILING INFORMATION

Navigation

Navigation around the islands and along the coast is predominantly of the eye-ball variety. The ancients navigated from island to island and prominent features on the coast quite happily and this is basically what yachtsmen still do in Greece. Eye-ball navigation is a much maligned art, especially now that electronic position finding equipment has arrived on the scene, but for the reasons outlined below it is still essential to hone your pilotage skills.

For good eye-ball navigation you need the facility to translate the two dimensional world of the chart into the three dimensional world around you. Pick out conspicuous features like a cape, an isolated house, a knoll, an islet, and visualise what these will look like in reality. Any dangers to navigation such as a reef or shoal water may need clearing bearings to ensure you stay well clear of them. Any eye-ball navigation must always be backed up by dead reckoning and a few position fixes along the way.Anyone with electronic position finding should exercise caution using it close to land or dangers to navigation. The paradox of the new equipment is that while you may know your position, often to an accuracy of 200 metres or less, the chart you are plotting your position on is not accurate in terms of its latitude and longitude. Most of the charts were surveyed in the 19th century using astronomical sights and the position of a cape or a danger to navigation, while proportionally correct in relation to the land mass, may be incorrect interms of its latitude and longitude. Some of the charts carry a warning, and corrections for latitude and longitude, usually the latter, of up to one mile! Consequently you are in the anomalous position of knowing your position to perhaps within 200 metres, but in possession of a chart which may have inaccuracies of a mile in its longitude. Blind acceptance of the position from electronic position finding equipment can and has lead to disaster.

Consistent winds and fairly flat seas make for good sailing in the Argolic.

Navigation and Piloting Hazards

The comparatively tideless waters of the Mediterranean, a magnetic variation of just over 2° (2°05'E 1990 (4'E)), and the comparatively settled summer patterns remove many of the problems associated with sailing in other areas of the world. Just having no tidal streams of any consequence to worry about enhances your sailing a hundred fold. Despite this there are hazards to navigation which while not specific to the Mediterranean, should be mentioned here.

Haze

In the summer a heat haze can reduce visibility to a mile or two which makes identification of a distant island or feature difficult until you are closer to it. Sailing from Athens down to Aegina or Poros you may not be able to positively identify features until you are three miles or so off. Approaching Athens the dreaded *nefos* caused by air pollution, at times worse than Los Angeles, can make identification of features difficult until you are two or three miles off. Heavy rain cleanses the air and dramatically improves visibility.

Sea Mist

In parts of the Aegean there may be a light radiation fog in the morning which can sometimes reduce visibility to a mile or less. The mist will gradually be burned off by the sun and by afternoon will invariably have disappeared.

Reefs and Rocks

The Saronic has only a few isolated dangerous rocks and reefs and with care these are normally easily spotted. However this absence of large areas of shoal water or extensive reefs can make the navigator lazy in his craft. The clarity of the water in the Mediterranean means you can easily spot rocks and shallows from the colour of the water. Basically deep blue is good, deep green means its getting shallow, lighter green means watch out, and brown lets you identify species of molluscs at first hand. However with a chop of any sort the whitecaps on the water can make identification of shallow water and reefs difficult and you should give any potential dangers a wide berth.

Fishing Nets

Care is needed around local fishing boats or in isolated bays where there may be surface nets laid. Vigilance is needed not to run over a net and incur not just the wrath of a fisherman, but most likely the net wrapped tightly around the propeller.

Lights

Although the islands and coast are quite well lit, the sheer extent of them means that it is impossible to light any but the most common routes used by ships and commercial fishermen. Navigation at night out of the common routes should be avoided unless you are familiar with the area.

Thunderstorm over the Peloponnese in the summer. Often these will come to nothing but at times a thunderstorm and an associated squall sweeps over the sea.

Winds

The winds in the Saronic are remarkably consistent in the summer. Details of the winds specific to the area are given at the beginning of each chapter but in general the area can be divided into two.

Along most of the Attic coast around Athens and down over the sea area east of Poros and Idhra the *meltemi* blows from the north-east. The *meltemi* begins fitfully in July and builds up to full strength through August and early September, dying down at the end of September. It will often blow up to Force 5-6 in this area and occasionally more. The *meltemi* tends to die off around Poros and Kolpos Idhras and to be funnelled in from the east. The *meltemi* will at times blow right down to Monemvasia and Cape Malea.

In Argolikos Kolpos and across to Idhra the prevailing wind in the summer is a sea breeze from the south-east which normally fills in around lunch time and dies down at night. It typically blows at around Force 4, sometimes a little less and sometimes a little more. The wind is reasonably reliable from June through to the end of September.

In the evening there may be a katabatic wind off the high mountains of the Peloponnese though there are only a few places, Astrous and Monemvasia are two, where you are likely to be affected by such a wind. On occasion the wind can get up to 30-35 knots though it is usually less and it generally lasts only a few hours before dying down. In the summer there may be isolated thunderstorms with an associated squall but these seldom last for more than a few hours and are normally over in less than an hour.

In the spring and autumn depressions passing north over the mainland or south around Cape Malea can give rise to strong southerlies or northerlies.

For more detail on the prevailing winds see the section at the beginning of each chapter.

Berthing

Berthing Mediterranean-style with the stern or bows to the quay can give rise to immense problems for those doing it for the first time, or even the second or third time. Describing the technique is easy: the boat is berthed with the stern or bows to the quay with an anchor out from the bow or stern respectively to hold the boat off the quay. It is carrying out the manoeuvre which causes problems and here a few words of advice may be useful, but will not replace actually doing it.

Everything should be ready before you actually start the manoeuvre. Have all the fenders tied on, have two warps coiled and ready to throw ashore with one end cleated off, and have the anchor ready to run, in the case of a stern anchor have the warp flaked out so it does not tie itself into knots as you are berthing. The manoeuvre should be carried out

Chaos in Idhra. In some of the harbours the sheer numbers of boats means that your anchor will inevitably foul or be fouled by another. Just patiently haul them up and untangle the mess.

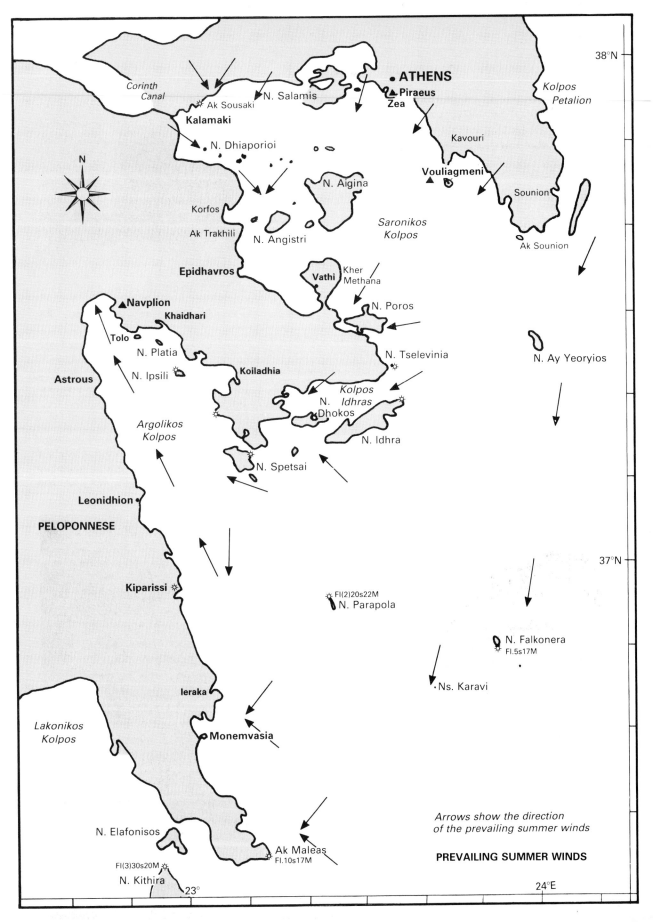

38°N

Corinth Canal

Kolpos Petalion

● **ATHENS**

▲ **Piraeus**

☼ Ak Sousaki **Zea**

Kalamaki N. Salamis

Kavouri

● N. Dhiaporioi

Vouliagmeni ▲

N

Korfos N. Aigina Sounion

Ak Trakhili *Saronikos Kolpos*

N. Angistri Ak Sounion

Epidhavros

Vathi Kher Methana

Navplion ▲ N. Poros

Khaidhari N. Tselevinia ☼

Tolo N. Ay Yeoryios

N. Platia *Kolpos Idhras* ☼

Koiladhia N. Dhokos ☼

Astrous N. Ipsili

Argolikos Kolpos N. Idhra

Leonidhion ● ☼ N. Spetsai

PELOPONNESE

Kiparissi ☼ 37°N

☼ Fl(2)20s22M
N. Parapola

N. Falkonera
☼ Fl.5s17M

Ieraka ●Ns. Karavi

Lakonikos Kolpos **Monemvasia**

Arrows show the direction of the prevailing summer winds

N. Elafonisos

Ak Maleas
Fl.10s17M

Fl(3)30s20M ☼ **PREVAILING SUMMER WINDS**
N. Kithira 23° 24°E

slowly using the anchor to brake the way of the boat about half a boat length off the quay. The anchor should be dropped about three or four boat lengths from the quay and ensure you have sufficient chain or warp beforehand to actually get there.

Many boats have a permanent set-up for going bows-to so there is not too much scrabbling around in lockers to extract an anchor, chain and warp. This can be quite simple: a bucket tied to the pushpit to hold the chain and warp and an arrangement for stowing the anchor on the pushpit. Boats going stern-to must have someone who knows what they are doing letting the anchor chain go. It should run freely until the boat is half a boat length off the quay. When leaving a berth haul yourself out with the chain or warp using the engine only sparingly until the anchor is up - it is all too easy to get the anchor warp caught around the propeller otherwise.

The Good Tourist

However much you hate being tagged with the label, we all are tourists, some longer term than others. If you like you can be the good holiday-maker, visitor, yachtsman, or whatever name that doesn't offend you. What is required of those of us who travel upon the water around the Saronic or anywhere else in the world for that matter, is that we do not stain the waters we travel upon or the land we come to. Some tourists regrettably seem not to have any understanding of the delicate relationship between tourist and locals and are so boorish and spend so much time whining about the faults of the country they have come to that I wonder why on earth they bothered - possibly because nobody in their own country could stand them. Which is not to say that the locals are angels. They can manage to emulate the worst of American and British excesses and can be as boorish as the worst of us, but then it is their country and so I suppose they have more license to do so. Local interaction aside, there are a number of substantive local complaints about us.

Although topless and bottomless sunbathing is tolerarted in places, don't flout it in villages and especially not near churches or monasteries. It is still technically illegal to discard all your clothes in Greece. Photo *Neville Bulpitt*.

Rubbish

Many of the smaller islands and villages are just not geared up to disposing of the rubbish brought in by tourists and on 'he water you will be visiting some small villages or deserted bays where there are literally no facilities at all. You should take your rubbish with you to a larger village or town and dispose of it there. Even the larger towns have questionable methods of disposing of rubbish and there is nothing wrong in trying to keep the number of convenience wrapped goods you buy to a minimum. My particular *bête noire* is bottled drinking water as the discarded plastic containers are to be found everywhere and when burnt (the normal way rubbish is disposed of on the islands) produce noxious gases and dangerous compounds.

It hardly needs to be said, you would think, that non-biodegradable rubbish should not be thrown into the sea. Even biodegradable rubbish such as vegetable peelings or melon rind should not be thrown into the water, except when you are five or more miles from land, or it ends up blowing back onto the shore before it has decayed or been eaten by scavengers. Toilets should not be used in harbour if there is one ashore, or they should be used with a holding tank. Holding tanks should not be emptied until you are well offshore.

I don't think most people can quarrel with the above, but sometimes I hear the argument that because the locals pollute the sea and the land, then why bother yourself. It is true that the locals are often the worst offenders, but consciousness of pollution and individual responsibility for it is spreading through the villages and towns and as tourists we have a responsibility to keep the wilder parts of Europe free from pollution when we have made such a tip of our own backyard. Moreover many of the sources of pollution are there to service the tourist trade and if there were no tourists then there would be less pollution.

Noise Pollution

This comes in various forms from the simple banality of making your presence known in an anchorage with the tape player turned up full blast to inconsiderate motor-boat owners with loud exhausts. Those who play loud music in deserted bays should reflect as to whether they would not be more comfortable in a noisy urban disco, preferably in their own country. Another annoying noise in an anchorage is the puttering of generators and those who need to run their generator all day and night might consider whether they may not be more comfortable in a marina where they can hook up to shore-power - there are a lot of nice marinas along the French and Italian Rivieras. Motor-boaters with noisy outboards and inboards, and water-bikes which somehow always contrive to have the most irritating whine in their exhaust note as well as the most irritating people driving them, should keep well clear of boats at anchor and keep noise levels to a minimum when they do come into an anchorage or harbour, or anywhere for that matter where they intrude on the peace and quiet most people, themselves included, come for.

Safety and Seamanship

In some places small powerboats and inflatables roar around an anchorage without regard for those swimming in the water. This is not just irritating but potentially lethal. If you have ever seen the injuries sustained by someone who has been hit by a propeller, you will immediately understand my concern. Accidents such as these frequently result in death or for the lucky, horrible mutilation. Those on large craft should also keep a good lookout when entering an anchorage where people are in the water or when their own crew is swimming off the back of the boat.

Remember when picking up someone who has fallen overboard to engage neutral or you may replace death by drowning with death by propeller injuries. Although water-bikes do not have a propeller they are just as lethal if they hit someone at speed and injure them - it doesn't take long to drown.

Conservation

Under the aegis of organisations like the World Wildlife Fund, Greenpeace, and Friends of the Earth, conservation is coming of age in Greece. A number of campaigns have been waged amongst them a campaign to step up measures against oil pollution and a campaign to reduce the amount of fertiliser and pesticides used in Greek agriculture. One of the problems in Greece is ensuring that action promised by the government is actually carried out and so far there has been little success. There is an awful short-sightedness in all this because failure to remedy environmental damage will have a catastrophic effect on the tourist industry in Greece and that would severely reduce already falling receipts from tourism.

Those sailing around should make sure they are fully paid-up to the environmental group of their choice and should themselves avoid polluting in any way the country they are in.

Weather Forecasts

Because of the high and large land masses in Greece it is extremely difficult to predict what local winds and wind strengths will be. The Greek meteorological service does its best but nonetheless faces an almost impossible task. Fortunately the wind direction and strength in the Saronic is remarkably consistent in the summer. For those who really want to listen to a weather forecast try the following sources, but remember to interpret them leniently.

Weather forecasts are transmitted on the National Programme. Only the 0630 forecast is in English, the other transmissions are in Greek only.

Local times
0630   Athens   729kHz   412m
(winter 0650)
2145 - 2200   Patras   1485kHz   202m

On Greek Public Television a weather forecast in Greek (but with synoptic charts and wind direction and force) is shown after the news at 2100 and 2200 local time on both Channel 1 and 2. In some of the *cafeneions* you will find a television you can watch over a beer or a coffee.

Quick reference guide

At the beginning of each chapter there is a summary of the information relating to the harbours and anchorages described. Compressing information into such a fixed framework is difficult and somewhat clumsy, but the list may be useful to some for route planning and as an instant memory aide to what a place offers.

Key
Shelter
A   Excellent all-round
B   Good with the prevailing winds
C   Reasonable shelter but sometimes dangerous
0   Calm weather only

Mooring
A   Stern or bows-to
B   Alongside
C   Anchored off

Fuel
A   On the quay
B   In the town
0   None

Water
A   On the quay
B   On the quay
0   None

Provisions
A   Excellent shopping
B   Most provisions available
C   Meagre supplies
0   None

Tavernas
A   Good choice
B   Some choice
C   One or two tavernas
0   None
Note This key applies to quantity not quality

Plan
▪   Harbour plan

About The Plans

The plans which accompany the text are designed to help those cruising in the area to get in and out of the various harbours and anchorages and to give an idea of where facilities are found. It is stressed that many of these plans are based on the authors' sketches and therefore should only be used in conjunction with the official charts. **They are not to be used for navigation.**

Key To The Symbols Used On The Plans

 : depths in METRES

 : shallow water with a depth of one metre or less

: rocks with less than 2 metres depth over them

: a shoal or reef with the least depth shown

⚓ (wreck symbol)	:	wreck partially above water
(breakwater symbol)	:	rock ballasting on a mole or breakwater
(rocks symbol)	:	above water rocks
(cliffs symbol)	:	cliffs
⚓	:	recommended anchorage
⚓	:	prohibited anchorage
⌖	:	church
⌐ ⌐	:	ruins
✗	:	windmill
□ □ □	:	houses
(castle symbol)	:	castle
(anchor in circle)	:	port police
(fish farm symbol)	:	fish farm
⚘	:	pine
(tree symbol)	:	trees other than pine
✉	:	post office
➘	:	telephone
ϟ	:	electricity
⚚	:	water
▮	:	fuel
O.T.E	:	Overseas Telecommunications Exchange
←—◆—|	:	yacht berth
(boats symbol)	:	local boats (usually shallow or reserved)
☼	:	light and characteristics
☼	:	lighthouse
F	:	fixed
Fl	:	flash
Fl(2)	:	group flash
Oc	:	occulting
R	:	red
G	:	green

W	:	white
M	:	miles
s	:	sand
m	:	mud
w	:	weed
r	:	rock

CHAPTER 1

THE ATTIC COAST

Corinth Canal to Sounion

	Shelter	Mooring	Fuel	Water	Provisions	Tavernas	Plan
Corinth Canal		B	O	O	O	O	▪
Isthmia	B	AB	O	O	O	C	▪
Ormos Kalamaki	C	C	O	O	C	C	
Salamis							
Ormos Salamis	B	AC	B	A	B	B	▪
Ormos Kanakia	C	C	O	O	O	O	
Ormos Seterli	C	C	O	O	O	O	
Ormos Peranis	C	C	O	O	O	C	
Zea	A	A	A	A	A	A	▪
Mounikhias	A	AC	B	A	B	A	▪
Faliron	B	A	B	A	A	A	▪
Kalamaki	A	A	A	A	B	B	▪
Glifadha 4	A	A	A	A	A	B	▪
Glifadha 1,2,3	A	A	A	A	A	B	▪
Voula	B	A	B	A	B	B	
Vouliagmeni	A	A	A	A	B	C	▪
Varkilas	B	A	B	A	B	C	▪
Ormos Anavissou	B	C	B	B	B	C	▪
Sounion	C	C	O	O	O	C	▪
Gaidhouromandra	B	A	B	A	O	C	▪

Mounikhias has a calm away from the noise and hectic activity of the rest of Athens-and good restaurants around the edge of the harbour to savour it in.

If ever a coastline was drenched in ancient history this is it. The obvious image of the Parthenon jumps out of every second postcard and travel brochure like a token of Greece itself. From Akrocorinth to the Temple on Sounion are names resonant with a roll-call of ancient battles, ancient seers and sages, heroes and tyrants, lovers and loveless suicide, names and monuments embedded in marble or lying in marble ruins on the ground. It is all too much. You can have ancient history and marble monuments with overkill. Even the dedicated philhellene will weary of it and seek refuge in a bar or taverna to escape the onslaught of old rock and ancient history. And in truth modern Athens and its environs has little to do with its ancient precursor.

After the Golden Age Athens declined in the Middle Ages to a dusty little village under the shadow of the Parthenon. It did not become the capital of a unified Greece again until 1834 and was not even the first nor the second choice for the base of the new government. The small village of perhaps a few thousand souls and the fishing village at Piraeus were catapulted to the centre of life and commerce in the newly unified Greece and the population exploded. Although some attempt was made at town planning, it did not touch the anarchy of the suburbs where houses and buildings were thrown together in a vast sprawl around the centre. It is this sprawl of uninspired buildings strung along the coast and around the centre that makes it difficult, almost impossible, to believe that Attica and Athens are at the root of what we like to call western civilisation.

Somehow we expect it to be different, to be an extension of the Parthenon, and when the awfulness of the place hits you it is like an assault on deeply held beliefs.

The geography of the coast is there and the place names as well, but all around the Attic coast the real symbols of western civilisation are obvious from the oil refinery belching noxious gases near Corinth through to the unbridled spread of reinforced concrete apartment blocks around Athens and its industrial suburbs to yet more reinforced concrete dotted with TV antennas spreading towards Sounion. Homer's wine dark sea is stained with industrial effluent and flotsam and jetsam of every description. On top of it all sits the dreaded *nefos*, the polluted cloud which hovers over the capital and on bad days is worse than anything Los Angeles can produce. All this needs to be said, especially for the first time visitor to the capital, who can be easily misled about the late 20th century presence of the city and its surroundings by books which dwell exclusively on the sights and ancient monuments without telling you what you've got to get through to get there. Once this is understood you can get down to enjoying what Athens has to offer as a bustling modern city with its ancient ruins as a bonus.

I am not going to dwell on what to see and do in Athens. The obvious things, the Parthenon and the other ancient buildings around it, the Archaeological Museum housing some of the finest ancient Greek sculpture in the world, the buzz of Plaka which was the original dusty village back in 1834, the cosmopolitan buzz of Syntagma and Ommonia, the evzones in white kilts and stockings with pom-pom shoes, a few meals and a few drinks, will occupy more than the few days anyone passing through on the water will stay here. If you are here longer there is a plethora of guide books on what to do and see and how to do so on sale in Athens.

Outside of Athens the Attic coast is nearly everywhere steep-to mountainous terrain except for the large nearly circular Attic plain on which the capital sits. Around the narrow coastal strip the suburbs of Athens have spread in an unbridled sprawl so that now modern Athens really extends from the industrial suburbs around Nea Perama to the far urban suburbs of Vouliagmeni and Varkilas. Today there are some three million living here, around one third the population of Greece, and it is still growing as the young, the ambitious, and the dispossessed home in on the magnetic attraction of a capital city. The infant industries of Greece have largely grown up here and it said that over 70% of all the industry in Greece is based around the perimeter of Athens, mostly around Elevsis and Perama. It certainly seems like it when you sail into the greeny-brown waters off Athens.

For water-borne travellers Athens is the yachting centre of Greece, the equivalent of the Riviera or the Solent. There are more yachts, private and charter, based here than anywhere else in Greece and all of them are chasing a permanent berth somewhere along the Attic coast. Of the nine marinas in Greece at the time of writing (not counting those under construction) six are clustered around Athens and they are all full to overflowing. Anyone bringing a yacht to Athens will have to be persistent and insistent if they are going to find a berth. Unless you are chartering a yacht from an Athens based company I personally think the best way to see Athens is by getting a ferry or hydrofoil from one of the nearby islands like Aegina or Poros where a yacht can be left safely for the day.

Getting Around Inland

For information on moving around Athens see the Introduction and simplified map of greater Athens for getting to and from the airport. Bus services run on regular routes: blue buses are the normal buses, yellow buses are express services, yellow trolley buses operate around the centre, and orange buses are from outside Athens. The underground runs virtually north to south through the city centre. Taxis are everywhere and so long as the meter is running are the easiest way to get about. Hire cars and motorbikes can be found everywhere.

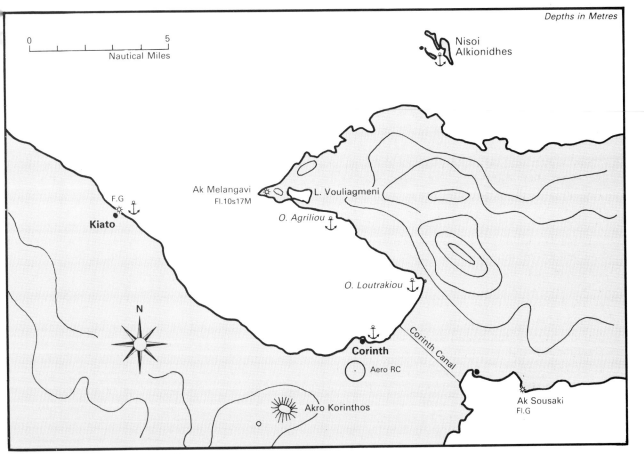

0   5
Nautical Miles

Nisoi
Alkionidhes

F.G
Kiato

Ak Melangavi
Fl.10s17M

L. Vouliagmeni

O. Agriliou

O. Loutrakiou

N

Corinth

Aero RC

Corinth Canal

Ak Sousaki
Fl.G

Akro Korinthos

APPROACHES TO CORINTH CANAL

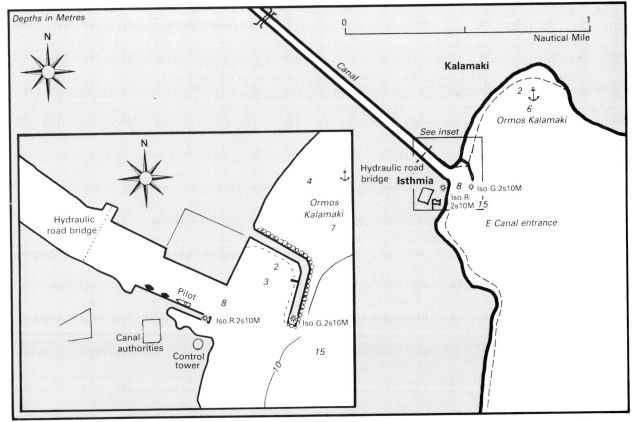

Depths in Metres

N

Canal

0   1
Nautical Mile

Kalamaki

2

6

Ormos Kalamaki

See inset

Hydraulic road
bridge

Isthmia

8   Iso G.2s10M

Iso.R.
2s10M   15

E Canal entrance

4

Ormos
Kalamaki

7

N

Hydraulic
road bridge

2

3

Pilot

8

Iso.R.2s10M

Iso.G.2s10M

Canal
authorities

Control
tower

10

15

CORINTH CANAL – EASTERN ENTRANCE

Corinth Canal

The idea of cutting a canal across the narrow waist connecting the Peloponnese to Attica was mooted by the ancient Greeks and many who came after. The present canal was started by the French and completed by the Greeks in 1893. It greatly reduces the distance between the Ionian and the Aegean and can be transited by yachts on payment of what is probably one of the highest canal fees per mile in the world.

The facts. The canal is just over three nautical miles long, 25 metres (81ft) wide, the maximum permitted draught is 7 metres (23ft) and the sides of the canal rise to 76 metres (250 ft) at the highest part of the cut. A current of 1-3 knots can flow in either direction depending on the direction and duration of the wind on either side and this can make passage through the canal difficult. I have encountered at least a 2 knot current which can make manoeuvring difficult. If you happen to be behind a large ship the wash from its and the attendant tugs propellers create a washing machine effect which can also cause problems when manoeuvring. Keep as far back from a ship in front as possible. There are mobile hydraulic bridges at either end which move a section to let yachts through.

At the western end of the canal (Posidhonia) the entrance is protected by breakwaters. IsoR2s10M and IsoG2s10M (stated range probably less) are exhibited at the entrance. In the summer westerlies often blow down onto the canal and the head of the gulf causing a lumpy swell. It is possible to anchor inside the southern breakwater but I don't recommend it as the holding is bad and the authorities are not happy about it. Just potter outside keeping the bows into the swell until the authorities signal you to enter.

At the Aegean end a breakwater protects a small harbour where you may find a berth or go along side on the quay by the Canal Authority building just inside the canal (Isthmia). All paperwork is carried out here and the canal fees must be paid before transiting through to Korinthiakos Kolpos or after coming through from the gulf. Care is needed when going alongside at Isthmia because of the rough concrete quay with reinforcing rods protruding in places and also for the wash from the pilot boats which enter and leave at speed. About half of the quay has been repaired with rubber fendering but at a difficult height for most yachts and care is still needed with fenders and springs.

The following signals for transiting the canal are displayed.

By day:	Blue flag	Entry permitted
	Red flag	Entry prohibited
By night:	Single white light	Entry permitted
	Two vertical white lights	Entry prohibited

The canal zone authorities use VHF channel 11. The canal is closed on Tuesday for repairs.

Caution Violent gusts can blow off the high land at either end of the canal. Both northwest and northeast winds gust off the land and as winds from these directions are common in the summer care is needed.

Note For pilotage and harbours down the Peloponnese coast and towards Aegina and Poros see Chapter 2. This chapter covers the Mainland coast to the east of the canal.

Ormos Kalamaki

The bay immediately north of the eastern end of the canal. There are numerous laid moorings in the bay for local boats so you need to anchor with care so as not to foul the ground tackle. Anchor in 4-10 metres on mud, sand and weed, mediocre holding so make sure your anchor is well in. Good shelter from northerlies although there are strong gusts into the bay off the hills. The bay is open to the south although southerlies are said not to blow home.

Tavernas ashore. The coast road from Athens to Corinth runs around the head of the bay and the rumble of traffic is incessant.

Corinth Canal looking east.

Ak Sousaki

Around the shores of the blunt cape there is a large oil refinery conspicuous by day because of its chimneys and by night by its flares. There are numerous jetties and quayed areas but this is no place for a yacht to be.

Nisos Salamis

Salamis is the largest island in the Saronic yet it is the least visited by land or water-borne travellers. One of the reasons it is little visited by yachts becomes obvious if you study the regulations prohibiting navigation and anchoring around the northern coast of the island. Add to this the islands proximity to the grubby industry on the nearby mainland coast and a relative lack of usable anchorages and its unpopularity is not too surprising. Perhaps also it is just too close to Athens and anyone leaving

the capital is more tempted by the other islands a little further away, Aegina and Poros, and the coast of the Peloponnese.

Despite the associations between the name of the island and the famous Battle of Salamis, there is little on the island to give you the feeling that here one of the decisive moments in ancient history was settled in favour of the Greeks and so enable the civilisation we base our own ideals on to continue to exist. For a summary of the essentials of the Battle of Salamis see the section in the introduction.

The island itself is arid in the north and east but well wooded in the southwest. It has a sizeable population, mostly in Salamis town, who are said to be predominantly of Albanian origin. There is a fair amount of agriculture on the island, numerous market gardens producing vegetables for Athens, and a growing number of pistachio groves following the success of pistachio cultivation on Aegina. On the northwest corner of the island is the monastery

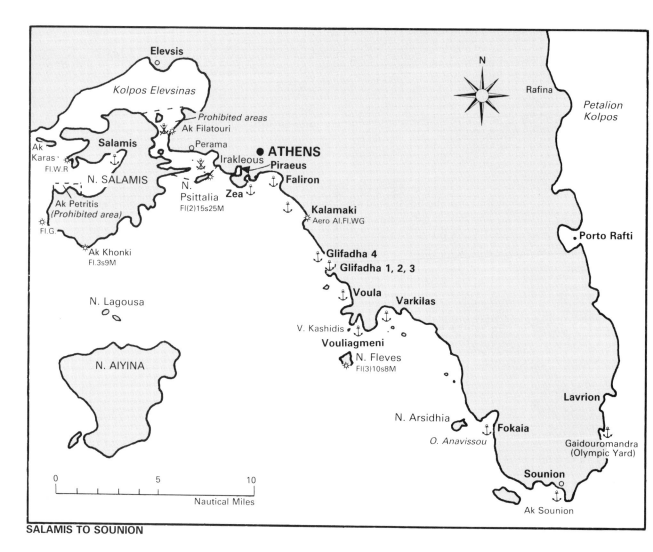

SALAMIS TO SOUNION

of Faneromeri, the Apparition of the Virgin, the centre of spiritual life on the island and a popular place of pilgrimage. Buses run from Salamis town if you want to visit it.

Getting Around

Buses run regularly from Paloukia, the ferry terminal on the east coast to Salamis town, the capital of the island. A less regular service run from Salamis to Faneromeni where an irregular ferry service operates to the mainland.

Regular ferries run from Paloukia to Perama on the opposite mainland shore. A less regular service operates from Paloukia to Piraeus. There is also a limited service from Faneromeni to Nea Perama.

Prohibited areas

1. In Ormos Salamis navigation is prohibited within half a mile of the shore between one and two miles east of Ak Petritis (the southern entrance point of the bay).
2. Navigation is prohibited around a small area off Elevsis in the northeast of Kolpos Elevsis.
3. Except for a narrow channel in the fairway, navigation is prohibited between the east side of

Nisos Salamis and the mainland coast opposite. Navigation at night is prohibited. Anchoring is prohibited everywhere in the channel between Nisos Salamis and the mainland from Perama to Kolpos Elevsinos.

Ormos Salamis

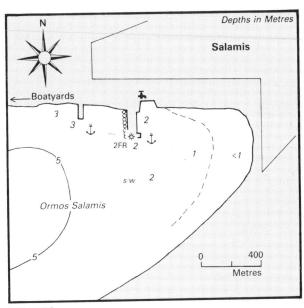

SALAMIS

Pilotage

Approach   The large bay on the west side of the island has no obvious distinguishing marks but the general location of the bay is easily ascertained. From the south the light structure on Nisis Kanakia will be identified when closer in. Once into the bay the cluster of houses of Salamis town will eventually be seen. When the *meltemi* is blowing there are gusts into the bay though little sea is generated across the bay.

Mooring   Anchor off the village in 2-5 metres or go stern or bows-to the short mole or off the short pier. These latter berths are usually crowded with fishing boats and you are unlikely to find a vacant spot. If you are going to the boatyard west of the town anchor off the yards in 4-10 metres. The bottom is mud, sand and weed, good holding once through the weed. Good shelter from the *meltemi* and open only to the south across the bay and to the west - westerlies are said not to blow home.

Facilities

Services   Water at the root of the mole and fuel in the town.

Provisions   Good shopping for provisions in Salamis town.

Eating Out   Tavernas in Salamis town and a taverna near the boatyards.

Other   Bank. PO. OTE. Ferry service from Paloukia to Perama and to Piraeus.

General

Salamis town, also known as Koulouri, cannot lay any claims to architectural distinction, but it has a dusty chaotic appeal to it and the locals are a friendly lot. In the town there is a small archaeological museum with some Mycenean artefacts recovered on the island.

Anchorages around the southwest end of Salamis

Ormos Kanakia The bay partially sheltered by Nisis Kanakia. In the approach care needs to be taken of the reef extending northwards from Nisis Kanakia and southwards for a shorter distance from the south of the islet. Anchor in the north or south part of the bay taking care of a reef fringing the shore in the middle part of the bay. Beach ashore and wooded slopes behind.

Seterli Just southwest of the hamlet of Seterli is a bay affording good shelter from the *meltemi*. Open west and south.

Ormos Peranis The large bay on the south side of Salamis. Care needs to be taken of the reef fringing the shore behind Nisis Pera in the bay. With strong winds from any direction some swell tends to roll into the bay. Some of the bay has now been developed as a sort of home-grown resort and there are tavernas on the beach in the summer.

Nea Perama to Perama

The mainland coast opposite the northern coast of Nisos Salamis is largely composed of industrial suburbs and is no place for a yacht to be. Unless you are going to the boatyards at Perama there is little point in entering this polluted stretch of water and there are no really good places for a yacht to bring up for the night.

If you want to explore the area where the Battle of Salamis took place take good care to stay out of the prohibited areas and in the channel permitted for navigation - I know of at least one yacht which was escorted out of the area when it strayed out of the permitted area.

Note Off the eastern end of Nisos Salamis and under Voi Skrofes and Nisis Atalandi and Nisis Psittalia are the anchorage areas numbers 1 and 2 for commercial vessels waiting to enter Piraeus. This cluster of ships at anchor is conspicuous in the approaches to Piraeus and the marinas around the coast when approaching from the south.

Piraeus

The commercial harbour of Piraeus is solely devoted to commercial shipping and the numerous ferries running to destinations all over the Aegean. A yacht should not make for the harbour and it is in any case usually suicide to do so with ships of all descriptions roaring in and out of the entrance at speed.

Zea Marina (Pasalimani)

Zea Marina sits just around the corner on the east side of the headland from Piraeus commercial harbour. It is difficult to pick out from the distance for the first time and you will need to concentrate on the various marks identifying bits of the skyline and the coast.

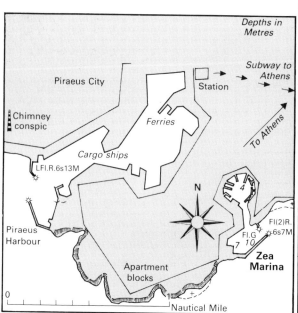

PIRAEUS – COMMERCIAL HARBOUR, ZEA AND TURKOLIMANI

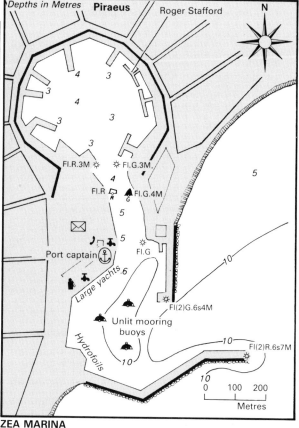

ZEA MARINA
37°56′N 23°39′·2E (Fl(2)R.7M)

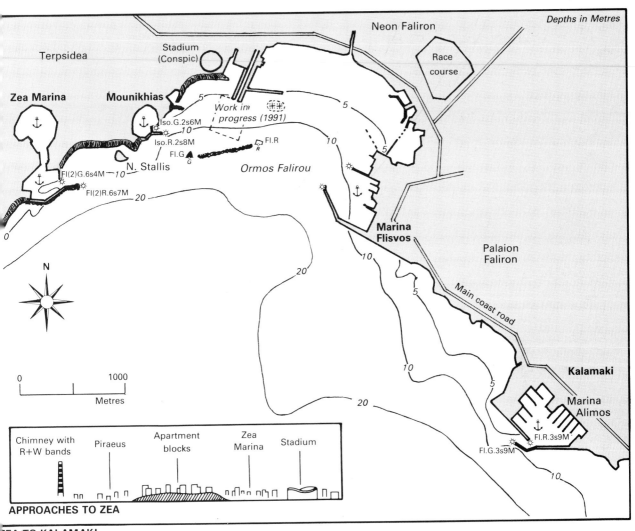

Depths in Metres

Terpsidea

Stadium (Conspic)

Neon Faliron

Race course

Zea Marina

Mounikhias

Iso.G.2s6M

Work in progress (1991)

Iso.R.2s8M

Fl.R

Fl.G

N. Stallis

Ormos Falirou

Fl(2)G.6s4M

Fl(2)R.6s7M

N

Palaion Faliron

Marina Flisvos

Main coast road

Kalamaki

Marina Alimos

Fl.R.3s9M

Fl.G.3s9M

0   1000

Metres

| Chimney with R+W bands | Piraeus | Apartment blocks | Zea Marina | Stadium |

APPROACHES TO ZEA

ZEA TO KALAMAKI

Pilotage

Approach   From the south and southeast the cluster of large ships at anchor off Piraeus commercial harbour will be seen and you need to keep a careful watch for ships getting underway from the anchorage or the commercial harbour. The blank wall of concrete of the apartment blocks spread along the coast makes it difficult to identify where exactly Zea is, but the sketch of the approach identifies the conspicuous objects on the skyline: the tall chimney at Piraeus and the stadium at Nea Faliron stand out well. The breakwater of the marina does not show up well, but once close in it will be seen as well the masts of yachts in the outer basin. Care is needed of hydrofoils entering and leaving the outer basin.

Mooring   If you have not already made prior arrangements for a berth you will usually be directed to a berth on the outer breakwater. Shelter in the inner basin is excellent but in the outer basin southerlies can cause a reflected swell which makes berths on the outer breakwater uncomfortable. Zea is a Port of Entry and if you want to obtain a Transit Log report to the marina office. Marina charges are made.

The entrance to Zea looking southwest from the coast

Facilities

Services Water and electricity at every berth. Shower and toilet block on the quay near the marina office. Fuel on the quay near the marina office.

Provisions Provisions and ice can be delivered to the boat. Good shopping for all provisions near the marina.

Eating Out Tavernas and restaurants of all types near the marina. You can eat Chinese, Italian, French or straight Greek. It is worth wandering around to *Mikrolimani* where you can eat well looking out over the small harbour.

Other Banks nearby. PO & OTE in the marina office. Doctors and dentists. Hospital. Hire cars and motorbikes. Ferries from Piraeus to most destinations in the Aegean. Hydrofoils from Zea to destinations in the Saronic and eastern Peloponnese.

General

Zea is one of the oldest small craft harbours, not just in Greece, but in the world. It was originally the harbour for ancient Zea and was ringed by some 196 ship-sheds. The inner circular basin was surrounded by a stone wall about 15 metres (50 ft) back from the water. A line of columns dividing the sheds off extended down to the water and the whole was roofed over. Slipways ran from the sheds into the water. Boats of this era were hauled regularly to dry out or they became so water-logged they could not be rowed or sailed. On a voyage the boats would be hauled onto a sandy beach, presumably on rollers and using manpower.

Only a few remains of the ship-sheds will be glimpsed amongst the subsequent rebuilding which has gone on at Zea. The inner circular basin is much the same as it was in ancient times but the outer basin is new and formerly the ancient harbour would have opened straight onto the sea.

Zea is arguably one of the best places to be close to Athens. It at least has the charm of being an established marina with all facilities nearby. It is easy to get into Athens from here and the streets behind the marina and over the ridge into Piraeus house shops and workshops selling and repairing just about anything you can think of. It is easy to spend half a day just wandering around and is usually more interesting than jostling with the crowds for a snapshot of the Parthenon. In the cinemas above the latest movies will be showing and these are usually sub-titled for Greece so that the original English dialogue remains.

Pasalimani the inner bassin of Zea.

Mounikhias (Turkolimani, Mikrolimani)

The almost circular harbour just east of Zea. It is administered by the Royal Hellenic Yacht Club and others and you should enquire in advance if a berth is available.

Pilotage

Approach The entrance lies ½ a mile ENE of Zea. The new detached breakwater just east of the harbour shows up well and closer in the masts of the yachts inside will be seen.

Mooring Berth where directed if you have permission. Numerous yachts are kept on fore and aft moorings in the middle of the harbour and navigating through them can be difficult. In calm weather it may be possible to go alongside the outer mole.

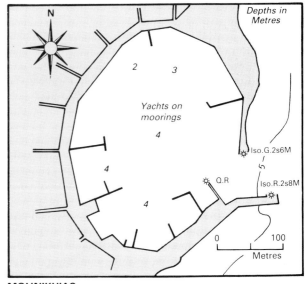

MOUNIKHIAS
37°56'·3N 23°39'·7E (Iso.R.8M)

Facilities

Water and electricity on the quay. Provisions nearby. The harbour is ringed by numerous and relatively expensive restaurants, many of which specialise in seafood. Yacht Club on the south side.

General

Like Zea this was also an ancient harbour surrounded by ship-sheds with slipways for an estimated 80 odd triremes. Originally two long moles provided additional protection with a lighthouse tower on the end of each. Parts of the ancient harbour can be seen around the present harbour and serving as the foundations for the present short moles at the entrance.

Although you are unlikely to find a berth here, the harbour is well worth a visit by land. Sitting in a natural amphitheatre by the sea it is something of an oasis away from the noise and frenetic atmosphere pervading most of Piraeus and Athens. Treat yourself to a meal looking out over the harbour and the sea beyond in an almost Italianate setting.

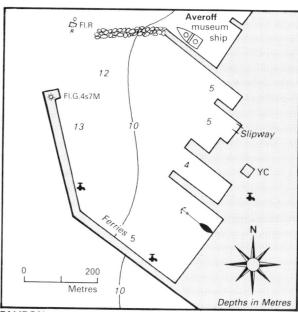

FALIRON
37°56′N 23°40′·8E (Fl.G.7M)

Mounikhias looking south from the slopes above.

Faliron (Phaleron, Flisvos)

The large harbour on the east side of Ormos Falirou.

Pilotage

Approach The outer breakwater is high and easily recognised. There are usually numerous large motor yachts (read small ships) berthed under the outer breakwater.

Mooring Go stern or bows-to where directed or where convenient. This is not really a harbour for a visiting yacht with most of the space occupied by permanent berth holders or reserved for the yacht club. A charge is made.

Facilities

Water and electricity on the quay. Good shopping and numerous tavernas and a very good *Pizzeria* nearby in Palaio Faliron.

General

It is a pity there are not more berths available here. You don't get the worst of aircraft taking off from the airport and are close to Palaio Faliron and its shops while not too far away is Athens centre. You will also be pleased to know there are no ancient bits of rock of consequence to see nearby.

Kalamaki (Alimos)

A comparatively new marina about 1½ miles southeast of Faliron harbour. It is usually very crowded with permanent berth holders and even they do not know if their own paid-up berth will be free when they return.

Pilotage

Approach The harbour blends into the coast and is difficult to identify from the distance. The buildings of the airport to the southeast and particularly a large blue hangar will be seen. From the west and southwest the green lawn of a cemetery with a conspicuous white cross immediately west of the marina will be seen. Closer in the masts of the yachts inside and the breakwaters can be identified. The entrance is not apparent until you are right up to it.

Kalamaki (Alimos) Marina

Mooring Finding a berth is something of a lottery. If you have chartered a boat here then shore staff will direct you to a berth which they guard jealously for their own and no other. Visitors berths are ostensibly under the west breakwater (berths A-E), but these are generally so congested with permanent berth holders that you will be lucky to find a

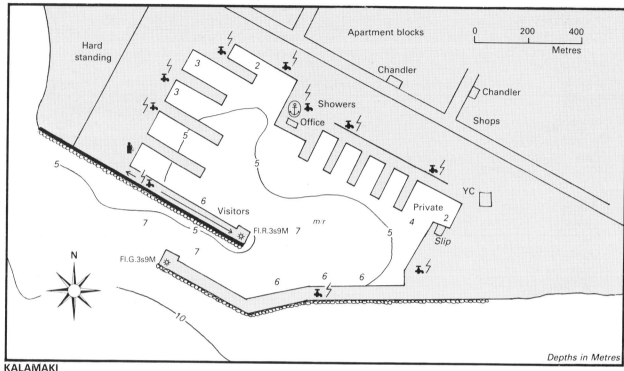

KALAMAKI
37°54'·8N 23°42'·1E (Fl.G.9M)

spot here. Just shove and push until you find somewhere. There are laid moorings for most berths but many have been cut or lost. The Marina Office is not generally helpful in sorting out a berth. Good all-round shelter. Marina charges are made.

Facilities
Services Water and electricity near every berth. Shower and toilet block near the office. Fuel On the quay. Yacht repair facilities.
Provisions Good shopping for provisions nearby on the main road. Provisions can be delivered to your yacht. A handcart and van come around with basic provisions and fruit and vegetables for sale in the summer. Ice available in the marina.
Eating Out A few tavernas and restaurants along the main road.
Other PO, OTE, and banks in Palaio Faliron. Hire cars and motorbikes. Buses into Athens.

General
Kalamaki is a convenient marina close to Athens, but more than that you cannot say. It is directly under the flight path of aircraft taking off or landing at the airport nearby and the din in the marina when a plane passes overhead is deafening. At night a disco in the marina puts out a decibel level that rivals the aircraft overhead. For charterers it is a convenient base to pick up a yacht but they should then head away from Kalamaki and Athens with all haste.

Glifadha 4

The first of the Glifadha marinas you come to heading down the coast from Athens.

Pilotage
Approach The marina is tucked into the north side of Ak Axionis. The buildings of the airport and the aircraft taking off and landing

give a clue to the general vicinity and closer in the masts of the yachts inside will be seen.
Mooring Go where directed by the marina attendant. There are laid moorings which must be picked up. Good all-round shelter. Marina charges are made.

Facilities
Services Water and electricity near every berth. Fuel delivered by mini-tanker. Shower and toilet block.

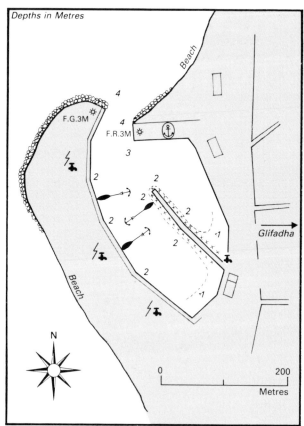

Depths in Metres

F.G.3M

F.R.3M

Glifadha

N

0   200
                Metres

GLIFADHA MARINA 4
37°52′·3N 23°44E (F.G.3m)

Glifadha 4 looking from the entrance

Provisions Good shopping for all provisions nearby in Glifadha. Some of the supermarkets will deliver to the boat. Ice available.

Eating Out Several restaurants near the marina and others in Glifadha. In my experience it is better to stick to those near the marina.

Other PO. OTE. Banks. Doctors. Dentist. Hire cars and motorbikes. Taxis. Regular buses into Athens on the main road nearby.

General

The marina is well run and efficient but suffers from the same blight as others along the coast. When aircraft are taking off and landing you cannot hear anyone speak and conversations between locals in Glifadha always have gaps in them where by habit they wait for the noise to finish before continuing with what they were saying.

Glifadha 1,2,3

The three small harbours just south of Glifadha 4. Although they are called marinas they are really much too small to merit the title.

Pilotage

Approach A church with a blue cupola on the shore and the masts of the yachts inside will be seen. Closer in a hoarding on the extremity of the mole of Glifadha 3 will be seen.

Mooring Go stern or bows-to where directed in Marina 3, the largest of the three small harbours. There are not normally berths available for visiting yachts. A charge is made.

Facilities

Services Water and electricity near every berth. Fuel in Marina 3.

Provisions Good shopping in Glifadha.

Eating Out Tavernas nearby and in Glifadha proper.

Other PO. OTE. Banks. Hire cars and motorbikes. Taxis. Buses into Athens from the main coast road.

General

The three small harbours are essentially private and in the summer you will have little chance of obtaining a berth. This is no great loss because like Glifadha 4 the noise from aircraft landing and taking off at the airport nearby is simply deafening.

Voula

A small harbour about a mile south of Glifadha 3. An L-shaped mole provides reasonable protection behind. Care is needed at the entrance which is fringed by above and below water rocks on the shore side. A small buoy marks the channel into the harbour. There are reasonable depths behind and a number of yachts are kept here permanently. Tavernas and shopping nearby.

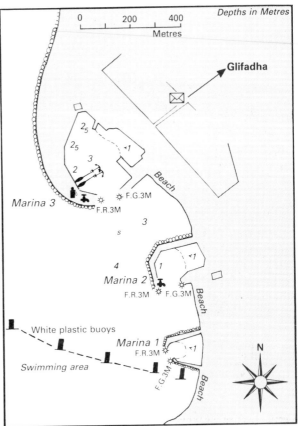

GLIFADHA MARINA (1, 2, 3)
37°51'·8N 23°44'·6E (Marina 3F.R)

Voula

Vouliagmeni

A marina tucked up on the west side of Ormos Vouliagmeni.

Pilotage

Approach Care needs to be taken of Vrakhonisos Kasidhis, an above water rock fringed by a reef lying off the western entrance point to the bay. There is an inside passage but the prudent course is to keep to seaward of it. A large white hotel on the slopes behind the marina is conspicuous and closer in the marina breakwater and the craft inside will be seen.

Mooring Berth stern or bows-to where directed by a marina attendant. There are laid moorings to be picked up and you should not use your anchor. In the summer the marina is packed full of permanent berth holders and you will frequently be turned away. Good all-round shelter although southerlies can cause a reflected swell which makes it uncomfortable. Substantial marina charges are made.

Facilities

Services Water and electricity near every berth. Fuel on the quay. Shower and toilet block ashore.

Provisions Most provisions available in Vouliagmeni proper at the head of the bay. Ice available.

Eating Out Several restaurants near the marina.

Other PO. OTE. Hire cars. Taxis. Bus service into Athens on the main road.

General

The marina was one of the first to be built in Greece and has a certain snobbish appeal situated next to the up-market real estate on the squiggly peninsula. It also has prices to match its 'appeal'. It does at least have the merit of being far enough away from the flight path into Athens Airport so that you can hear yourself speak.

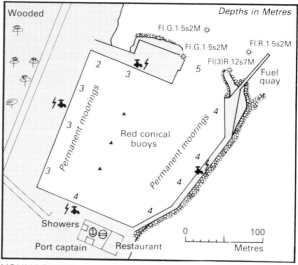

VOULIAGMENI
37°48'·3N 23°46'·6E (Fl.R.2M)

Ormos Vouliagmeni

A yacht can anchor near the head of Ormos Vouliagmeni where there is good shelter from the *meltemi*. It is open to the south.

Varkilas

A small harbour in Ormos Varis, the large bay east of Vouliagmeni.

Pilotage

Approach In Ormos Varis, Pondikonisi (Mouse Island) and the two rocks, Vrakhonisos Lito and Artemis, are easily identified. The harbour lies in the northwest corner of the

Vouliagmeni looking south towards the entrance

bay. Care is needed of the underwater rocks around the end of the breakwater.

Mooring Go stern or bows-to the outer mole or berth inside if there is room. Care is needed on the outer mole of the ballasting which extends underwater in places. In the inner basin local fishing boats usually occupy most of the berths in the southern corner and local boats are kept on the pontoon.

Facilities

Services Water on the quay. A mini-tanker can deliver fuel to the quay.

Provisions Good shopping for provisions near the harbour.

Eating Out Tavernas nearby and on the beach.

Other PO. Taxis and buses into Athens.

General

There is nothing special to bring you here to this outer suburb of Athens. The wide coast road runs behind the harbour and on the other side are the blank apartment blocks almost synonymous with an Athenian suburb. For all that there is nothing to really to drive you away either.

Varkilas looking out from the inner basin

Vrakhoi Koudhounia

The above water rocks and reef and shoal water extending out from the coast about one mile north of Nisis Arsidha. The reef and shoal water extend in a ESE direction from the coast for one mile so considerable caution is needed. A yacht should keep well to seaward. Although there is an inshore passage it is not recommended.

Ormos Anavissou

The large bay east of Nisis Arsidha.

Pilotage

Approach Nisis Anavissou is easily identified and the channel between it and the coast has adequate depths. The above water rock approximately in the middle of the channel is easily identified. In the entrance to the bay the village of Palaia Fokaia will be seen.

Mooring There are several places a yacht can anchor around the bay.

VARKILAS
37°49′·1N 23°48′·3E (F.R.3M)

Depths in Metres

Apartment blocks

Coast road

N

Local boats

Pontoon

m/r/w

Fishing boats

F.R.3M

0   50

Metres

ORMOS ANAVISSOU
37°43'·2N 23°56'·7E (F.G.3M)

1. On the west side of the bay. The *meltemi* tends to blow into here and it is not really a good place to be.
2. In the northwest corner where a number of local boats are kept on permanent moorings. Here there is better shelter from the *meltemi*.
3. Off Palaio Fokaia. The small harbour has inadequate depths for a yacht and you should not attempt to enter it or berth here. Anchor off the harbour in 3-5 metres. The bottom is partially composed of jagged coral-like rock

Palaio Fokaia in Ormos Anavissou

that can snag an anchor so use a trip line or potter around until you find a patch clear of rock. The *meltemi* gusts off the land but there is adequate shelter here.

In the village ashore fuel is available and there is good shopping for provisions. Several tavernas close to the harbour. This is really the first place where you feel that you have left Athens and are in the country although the coast road nearby is still fairly busy.

The passage inside Gaidhouronisi. Care is needed of the reef about ½ a mile off the mainland

Nisos Gaidhouroniso

A high bold island lying ¾ of a mile off the coast 3 miles west of Ak Sounion. There are adequate depths in the fairway between the island and the coast but care is needed of the reef lying ½ a mile off the mainland coast at the eastern end of the channel. Reefs also border the mainland coast for some distance at the eastern end of the channel.

Sounion

The cape on the southeast corner of the Attic coast. It is commonly used by yachts waiting to go across to the Cyclades or back up towards Athens.

Pilotage

Approach The temple on the top of Ak Sounion is conspicuous from nearly everywhere. Closer in the islet of Arkhi in the entrance to the bay will be seen.

Mooring Anchor in the cove under the temple where convenient. The bottom is hard sand and weed, bad holding in most places and you should ensure your anchor is well in and if in doubt lay a second anchor. Good shelter from the *meltemi* although there are strong gusts into the bay. There are two mooring buoys in the cove although it is not certain why they are there - it may be worth taking a warp to one. If the cove is crowded yachts also anchor in the north of the bay and in fact all round the bay in the summer.

Facilities

Several tavernas ashore.

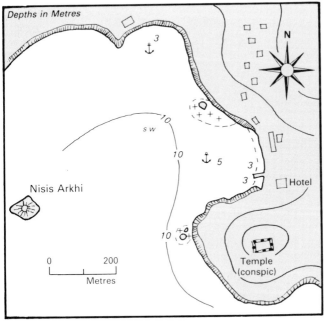

Sounion. The cove under the temple.

General

The temple on the cape is wonderful, an evocative place- and evidently most tourists in the vicinity of Athens think so if the numbers of coaches lining the road in the summer are anything to go by. From lunch time right up to sunset coaches rumble to and from the cape and the temple. Luckily those travelling by water can nip up in the morning before the first coaches arrive and savour the atmosphere in comparative solitude.

The Temple to Poseidon was built around 444 BC and stands on the foundations of an older temple. The temple did not exist in isolation but was linked to the small city of Sounion at the head of the bay. It was a wealthy little place with proceeds from the ships which stopped in here to shelter from the *meltemi* just as yachts do today. Grain ships bound for Piraeus from Evia would put in here regularly and ships working their way from the Cyclades towards Piraeus would also stop here for a breather.

Sounion was evidently something of a tearaway city. Its wealth was legendary in the ancient world. It had a reputation for looking after runaway slaves without too many questions being asked. Later it was a refuge for corsairs and pirates. It was here that William Falconer was wrecked in a Levantine trader

SOUNION
37°39′N 24°01′·5E

The Temple of Poseidon on Cape Sounion. The Greeks
located it with their usual flair, Falconer was ship-wrecked
in its shadow and Byron carved his name on a column.
Evocative it certainly is and much visited because of that.

and so acquired the material for his poem *The
Shipwreck*. Falconer was both sailor and poet
and an adventurer as well. He went to sea as a
boy and though he wrote numerous poems, only
The Shipwreck published in 1762 was popular.
Later Falconer moved from the Merchant Navy
to the Royal Navy and published *An Universal
Dictionary of the Marine* in 1769, the same year
he was drowned at sea. This extract tells of the
fatal impact of the ship on Cape Colonna as
Sounion was then called.

"By now Athenian mountains they descry,
And o'er the surge Colonna frowns on high;
Where marbled columns, long by time defaced,
Moss-covered on the lofty Cape are placed;
There reared by fair devotion to sustain
In elder times Tritonia's sacred fane;
The circling beach in murderous form appears,
Decisive goal of all their hopes and fears:
The seamen now in wild amazement see
The scene of ruin rise beneath their lee;
Swift from their minds elapsed all dangers past,
As dumb with terror they behold the last."

It behooves me to mention that Byron also
visited here and carved his name on a column,
an act of vandalism that draws many to the cape
to see where the bard visited. Now the temple

proper is fenced off to stop the erosion caused by countless feet wandering around it you will not actually see it, but don't let that put you off visiting it in the early morning. The temple is also at one corner of the giant isosceles triangle formed by Sounion, Aphaia on Aegina, and the Parthenon, temples all built around the same time - a surveying feat of some magnitude.

Gaidhouromandra (Olympic Marine Yard)

An inlet just around the corner from Sounion occupied by the Olympic Marine Yard.

Pilotage

Approach From the south the inlet and the boatyard are difficult to identify until you are around Ak Fonias and at the entrance. Once

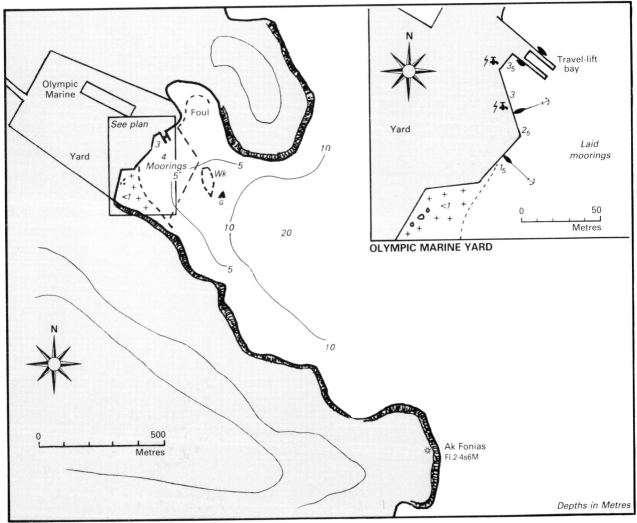

GAIDHOUROMANDRA (OLYMPIC MARINE)
37°41′·8N 24°03′·7E

there the yachts hauled out onto the hard and the hangar-like buildings of the yard will be seen. Care must be taken of the wreck in the bay marked only by a small conical green buoy. The latter is not always in place and care is needed when navigating in the bay.

Mooring Craft are kept on permanent moorings in the bay and you will need to wend your way through them to the quay. Only part of the quay is suitable for craft to go stern or bows-to as the rest is shallow and rocky. A charge is made.

Facilities
Services Water and electricity on the quay. Showers and toilets. Fuel can be delivered. Extensive yacht repair facilities.
Provisions Nearby in Lavrion. A market on Thursday.

Eating Out Foti's taverna at the yard is good value. Otherwise tavernas in Lavrion.
Other Telephone and fax services. Taxis. Infrequent bus service to Athens.

General
The yard is the most extensively equipped near Athens and consequently is popular for hauling and refitting. Its drawback is that it is really in the middle of nowhere with poor public transport to and from Athens.

Gaidhouromandra and the Olympic Yard looking from the south side of the bay.

Passage to the Cyclades

From Sounion many yachts will head across to Kea or Kithnos or further over to Siros or Mikonos. In the summer with the *meltemi* this means a brisk reach if you are lucky or more likely a wet ride under much reduced sail. The *meltemi* tends to howl down through the Kea Channel and over Kea and Kithnos. A confused sea is inevitably set up and for some charterers this is enough of an introduction to the *meltemi* at full blast and they then head west until it begins to peter out.

Charter boats which continue on downwind should remember they will have to bash back against the *meltemi* if the boat is based around Athens and this can mean a wet and miserable end to a sailing holiday. At one time I made a living bringing charter boats back to Athens from the Cyclades in the *meltemi* season, but it is not something I would do again. There are better things to do than bashing back against the *meltemi* through the upper Cyclades. One tip: you can always head west towards Poros and then power up to Athens when the *meltemi* drops in the early morning.

CHAPTER 2

AEGINA TO POROS

And The Adjacent Coast

	Shelter	Mooring	Fuel	Water	Provisions	Tavernas	Plan
Ormos Kenkhreon	O	C	O	O	O	O	
Ormos Linari	O	C	O	O	O	O	
Ormos Frangolimani	O	C	O	O	O	O	
Ormos Dimani	O	C	O	O	O	O	
Nisoi Dhiaporoi	O	C	O	O	O	O	
Korfos	A	AC	B	B	B	B	▪
Ormiskos Selonda	B	C	O	O	O	O	
Nea Epidhavros	O	C	O	O	C	C	
Palaia Epidhavros	B	AC	B	A	B	B	▪
Psifti	O	C	O	O	O	O	
Isthmus Bay	C	C	O	O	O	O	
Ormos Pounda	C	C	O	O	O	O	
Vathi	A	A	O	B	C	B	▪
Chapel cove	C	C	O	O	O	O	
Kounoupitsa	O	AC	O	O	O	C	
Methana	A	A	B	A	A	B	▪
Aegina							
Aegina harbour	A	A	A	A	A	A	▪
Souvalas	C	A	O	O	C	C	▪
Aghia Marina	O	C	O	O	O	C	
Ormos Kipos	C	C	O	O	O	O	
Ormos Pirgos	C	C	O	O	O	O	
Perdika	B	AC	O	A	C	B	▪
Nisis Moni	C	C	O	O	O	C	
Anghistri							
Skala Anghistri	C	AC	O	B	C	B	▪
Dhoroussa anchorages	C	C	O	O	O	C	
Poros							
Poros harbour	A	A	A	A	A	A	▪
Ormos Vidhi	C	C	O	O	O	O	
Ak Dana	C	C	O	O	O	O	
Russian Bay	B	C	O	O	O	O	
Ormos Neorion	B	C	O	O	C	C	
Ormos Aliki	C	C	O	O	O	C	
Ormos Askeli	O	C	O	O	O	C	
Monastery Bay	C	C	O	O	O	C	
Ormos Barbaria	C	C	O	O	O	O	

Vathi on Methana

Perdika on Aegina

This chapter covers the western side of Saronikos Kolpos, (the Saronic Gulf), and is the area where most yachts based in Athens make for if they are not off to the Cyclades. Consequently the stretch of water between Athens and Aegina and Poros is frequently busy at the weekends and all through August. Surprisingly there are still some tranquil and uncrowded places, mostly along the coast of the Peloponnese, off what charter skippers here call the "milk run".

The coast of the Peloponnese is mostly steep-to, rising straight up from the sea to a jumble of mountainous ridges that criss-cross the area with no apparent pattern. The highest peak near the coast is Ortholithi, opposite the peninsula of Methana, rising to 1115 metres (3625 ft). Most of the other peaks are around 600 to 900 metres (2000 to 3000 ft). While the upper slopes are barren and rocky, indeed forbidding in places, the lower slopes are often covered in pine. The main islands of Aegina and Poros are lower gentler places making them more amenable to agriculture, principally those two mainstays of the Mediterranean, the olive and the grape. In recent years the area of land cultivated for the vine has decreased and wine is now largely imported from the mainland. The olive has also declined because collecting the olives is so labour intensive compared to collecting money from the ample crop of tourists in the summer.

As might be expected of an area this close to Athens, there are rich historical associations. Troezen on the mainland opposite Poros was readied for the evacuation of Athens when Xerxes looked like he would crush the Athenian forces. Ancient Aegina was once a prosperous trading centre and aroused the envy and wrath of Athens. Epidavros was the centre of ancient medicine and bequeathed a lesson in acoustics to our high-tech age in the shape of its perfect theatre. Aegina was the first capital of newly liberated Greece in 1833. Yet strangely enough it all feels a lot further from the glories of ancient Athens and the smog and pollution of modern Athens than the actual sea miles suggest. At least for the latter that is a blessing.

Prevailing Winds

The prevailing summer winds in this area vary considerably. In Kolpos Kenkhreon west to northwest winds often blow out from the Gulf of Corinth. These can be strong at times and often there are severe gusts off the coast of the Peloponnese down to Epidhavros. When the *meltemi* is blowing the wind is northeast down over Aegina and Anghistri and curves to the east around Poros.

This area is on the limit of the *meltemi* and although it can sometimes blow strongly, it often dies out by mid-afternoon when a southerly sea breeze fills in. In the sea area between Aegina and Poros you will often be caught between the receding northeasterly and the advancing southeasterly.

There will sometimes be thunderstorms and an associated squall, though these are comparatively rare in summer.

Looking across to Methana peninsula from the steep-to slopes of the Peloponnese.

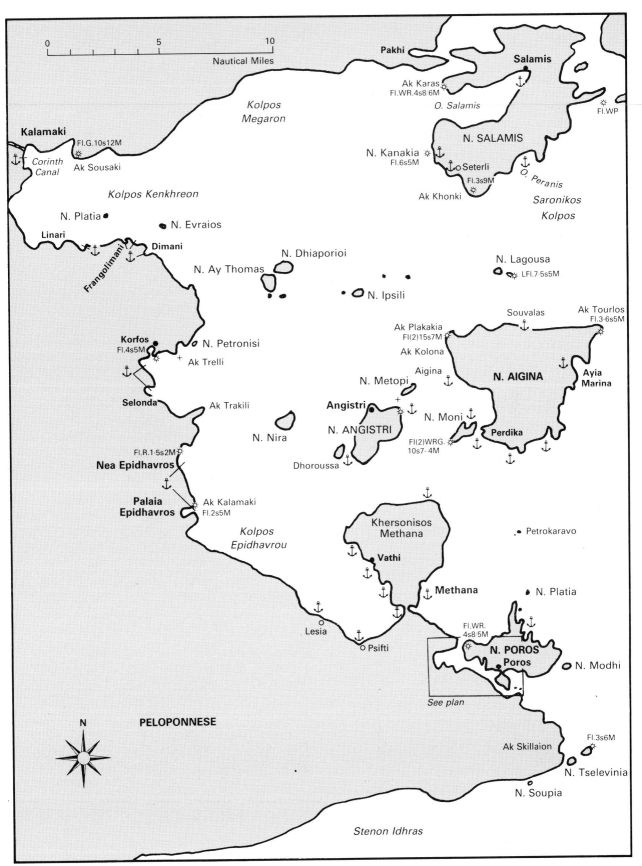

CORINTH CANAL TO POROS

Ormos Kenkhreon

The large bay two miles south of the Corinth Canal. It can be used in calm weather or in the westerlies which sometimes blow out of the Gulf of Corinth. Anchor in 3-10 metres where convenient on sand and weed.

It is here that ancient Corinth's second port, Kenkhreai, was built and parts of it remain on the sea bottom. There is some confusion over whether boats were loaded here to be dragged across the *diolkhos* or whether they were loaded at Kalamaki to the north of the present entrance to the canal. Ashore there are salt water springs where allegedly Helen of Troy once bathed so not surprisingly they are called Helen's Baths.

Ormos Almiri

The large bay immediately south of Kenkhreon. Suitable in calm weather or westerlies.

Ormos Linari

Affords some shelter from the east and south but shelter is not as good as it looks on the chart. It is also deeper than shown.

Ormos Frangolimani

Affords some shelter from the east and south but like Linari shelter is not as good as it looks. With easterlies a reflected swell enters. It is deeper than shown and you will usually have to anchor in 10 to 15 metres with a line ashore.

Ormos Dimani

A bay about one mile ESE of Frangolimani. It affords some shelter from westerlies.

Around the slopes of these three bays villas are being built-presumably for affluent Athenians for whom it is a short drive from the capital.

Nisidhes Platia and Evraios

Neither of these two islets in Kolpos Kenkhreon have usable anchorages. Platia has a fish farm on its southern side.

Ormos Kirkati

A bay lying approximately two miles SE of Dimani. Suitable in calm weather although it is quite deep for anchoring.

Nisoi Dhiaporoi

The group of islands lying three miles east of Kirkati. There are two major islands: Nisos Ay Ioannis and Nisos Ay Thomas. The channel between the two islands has less depth than shown on the charts with a reef connecting the two islands and only 3-4 metre depths closer to Ay Ioannis. Passage between the islands is possible in daylight but have someone up front conning you through

There are two anchorages. On Ay Ioannis a yacht can anchor off on the east side though it is only really tenable in calm weather. On the south side of Ay Thomas a yacht can tuck under the chapel to get some protection from the *meltemi*

Nisidhes Ipsili, Stakhtorroi and Platia

This group of three islets lie east of Nisoi Dhiaporoi and off the northwest corner of Aegina. There are no anchorages and in any case Nisis Ipsili is used for target practice by the Greek navy. Already half of the islet is said to have been destroyed so I suggest you stay well clear, especially if a few dull grey ships appear over the horizon moving at speed. I was once escorted out of the area by two destroyers during a combined forces exercise (it started just as I was passing Ipsili) and I hope it is the nearest I ever get to a military operation.

Korfos (Limin Sofikou)

The large bay tucked around the corner from Ak Trelli. The houses of the village will not be seen until you are up to the entrance to the bay.

Pilotage

Approach There is little to indicate exactly where the bay is but its general position is obvious. Nisis Petronisi and Nisis Kira are easily identified. From the north considerable care is needed of the reef running out from Ak Trelli for nearly a quarter of a mile. Its danger is compounded by the fact that Ak Trelli itself is very low so it is difficult to see where the reef begins - give it a wide berth. Once up to the entrance of the bay the houses of the village will be seen and entry is straightforward.

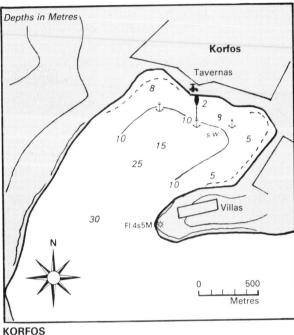

KORFOS
37°45'·5N 23°07'·7E (Fl.4s5M)

Korfos. With care you can go on the quay, otherwise anchor off.

Mooring Anchor where convenient. The bay is quite deep for anchoring and you will probably be dropping the anchor in 10-15 metres. A yacht can also go bows-to the quay off the village though care is needed as ballasting extends out in places - reconnoitre first to be sure there are sufficient depths. The bottom is mud and weed, patchy holding in places. There is good all-round shelter bay although with westerlies there are strong gusts off the high land into the bay.

Facilities

Services Water from a taverna if you can get onto the quay. Fuel available.

Provisions Most provisions can be found nearby.

Eating Out Several tavernas along the waterfront which is quite the most pleasant place to be. *Georges* taverna on the waterfront is well known to yachties cruising around here.

Other PO. Metered telephone.

General

The village is a nondescript sprawl of careless reinforced concrete houses, many of them left in the usual unfinished fashion with reinforcing rods pointing skywards, a ploy that avoids the tax on roofs. The slopes about the village are rough folded rock covered in *maquis* and stunted pine bent by the westerlies which often howl off the hills. Despite the stunted architecture that goes with the pines, the waterfront is a convivial intimate place and one which grows on you the longer you stay.

Ormiskos Selonda

A deep inlet nearly two miles south of Korfos. The deep slit in the hills is reasonably easy to identify. The inlet is now partially obstructed by a fish farm but there is still room to anchor, although it is quite deep. Good shelter from all but easterlies. Even with the fish farm here this is a peaceful spot.

Nea Epidhavros

Off the village in Ormos Nea Epidhavrou (New Epidhavros) there is a short pier but depths off it are barely 1-1.5 metres and you are better off anchoring in the bay. There is not a lot of shelter to be gained here and a boat should not be left unattended.

Taverna ashore. The bay is an attractive place and in calm weather makes a good lunch stop.

Palaia Epidhavros

The village of Old Epidhavros (although most of it is in fact newer than New Epidhavros) lies tucked into a bay and out of sight from seawards. It is the logical place to make for to arrange an excursion to Epidhavros theatre and the Askeplion.

Pilotage

Approach The exact location of the bay is difficult to see from seawards but a road scar south of the bay will be seen and closer in the light structure and a chapel on the north side of the bay. Once in the entrance to the bay everything falls into place: the buildings of the village will be seen and the two beacons marking the channel into the harbour are easily identified.

Mooring Go bows or stern-to the quay or anchor off where shown. The bottom is mud and some weed, generally good holding. Good protection from most winds. The bay is open east, and although the wind does not blow home it sends a swell in.

Facilities

Services Water on the quay. Fuel can be delivered by mini-tanker.

Provisions Good shopping for provisions in the village. Ice available.

Eating Out Numerous tavernas near the harbour and in the village. There is a good *souvlaki/kokoretsi* taverna in the main street and good pizzas near the waterfront.

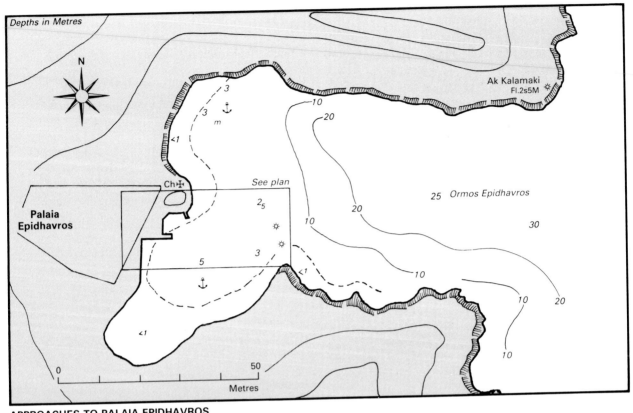

Depths in Metres

N

Ak Kalamaki
Fl.2s5M

Ch ⊕

Palaia
Epidhavros

See plan

25 Ormos Epidhavros

30

0   50
Metres

APPROACHES TO PALAIA EPIDHAVROS

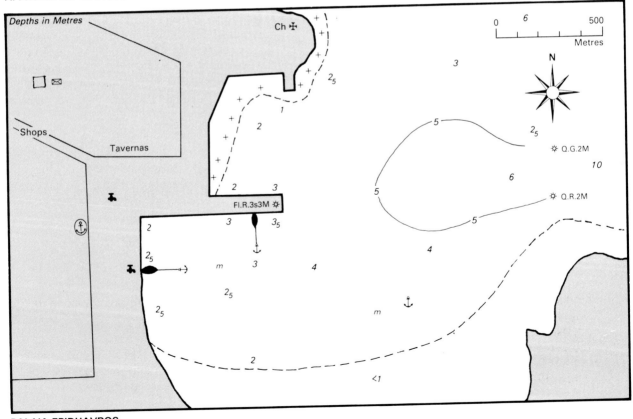

Depths in Metres

Ch ⊕

0   6   500
Metres

N

Shops

Tavernas

Q.G.2M

Fl.R.3s3M ☼

Q.R.2M

PALAIA EPIDHAVROS
37°38'·3N 23°09'·5E (Fl.R on quay)

Epidhavros looking out over the bay. Note the beacons marking the channel.

vendors, stalls selling votive offerings, entertainers, indeed anything on which a drachmae or two profit could be made from the pilgrims.

In the Roman era the Askeplion was more akin to a health farm than a temple of healing and literally thousands arrived during the great festivals held in the theatre - it is difficult to imagine the little harbour crowded with ships and the hustle and bustle in the village and on the road leading up the gorge.

Epidhavros. The town quay.

Other Bank. PO. OTE. Hire motorbikes. Taxis who will usually tout around the harbour for excursions to Epidhavros theatre.

General

Though it is called "old" Epidhavros, the hamlet at the head of the inlet is anything but old - a huddle of reinforced concrete houses, hotels, tavernas, bars and souvenir shops. In an attempt to tidy the place up the local council has constructed a strip of garden along the harbour front, presumably to hide the buildings. The "old" tag refers of course to the Askeplion and theatre inland from the harbour.

It was here the patients and visitors to the Askeplion would arrive. From here it was normally a two day trip up the steep winding gorge behind and into the valley of Epidhavros and the promised cure, around 12 kilometres altogether. Some would have travelled by donkey and some by sedan chair, but the majority would have walked, up through the steep gorge. Along the way hostels and pilgrims rest-places have been excavated and we can assume there were tavernas and fast-food

Epidhavros

Most people have heard of Epidhavros theatre. Its acoustics are legendary and everyone has heard the stories of how a piece of paper rustled or a coin dropped in the orchestra can be clearly heard in the top row of seats 22½ metres (74 ft) from the orchestra. The stories are true and there is no doubt the acoustics are as near perfect as you can get for an outdoor stone construction. But in ancient times Epidhavros was not famed for its theatre but as a place of healing.

At Epidhavros the simple rites of healing took the first steps towards systemic medicine. We know little of the ritual healing which took place here and to some extent must guess at what went on. Patients were first induced into a sleep, perhaps with the use of drugs burnt in vessels, and then left for varying periods until the sleep therapy (*encoemesis*) was deemed to have done its job. It is likely that some form of hypnotism or mesmerism was used as appears to have been the case at the Temple to Hemithea in Asia Minor which had a good success rate reducing pain during childbirth. This sort of holistic approach to healing can accomplish minor miracles and it is only now, a few thousand years later, that we are beginning to appreciate the power of mind over body and the body's own curative powers.

Empirical techniques were also used at Epidhavros. Frequent washing of the body was prescribed and old clothes, crutches, walking sticks and the like could not be brought into the sanctuary. Medical historians will tell you that simple hygiene practices are the greatest step forward in medicine we have ever made. Diet and hydrotherapy were also considered important and the water at Epidhavros, like that at Lourdes, is still considered to have curative properties even if it does come out of an old tap. Some surgery was carried out at Epidhavros such as the opening of the abdominal cavity to remove parasites (recorded on a stele found nearby), but this was the exception rather than the rule.

Of Askeplius himself we know little. He seems to have been deified after birth and his genealogy smoothed out once he became popular. He probably lived around the 13th century BC and was later said to be the son of Apollo and Koronis. His symbol was the staff with a snake entwined about it and according to some experts this is the harmless grass snake and not a poisonous species. The symbol is the one still used by the medical profession today. At first Askeplius was a local deity of Epidhavros and Thessaly, but as the fame of Epidhavros grew as a centre of healing his influence spread and it is likely that his subsequent deification occurred around this time.

The foundations of the Temple of Askeplius where the treatment took place, various other temples, baths, the gymnasium, and the Katagogion (probably a hotel) are there. Only the theatre remains largely intact.

It was designed by Polycleites the Younger and built in the 4th century BC. It seats 14000 in 55 rows of seats arranged in a semi-circle around the orchestra. Apparently the angle of incline of the theatre, around 26.5:1, provides the optimum angle for sound-waves to reach the top row of seats without any significant reduction in strength. Hitler copied the design of the theatre for the Olympic Games in Berlin in 1936.

Epidhavros theatre.

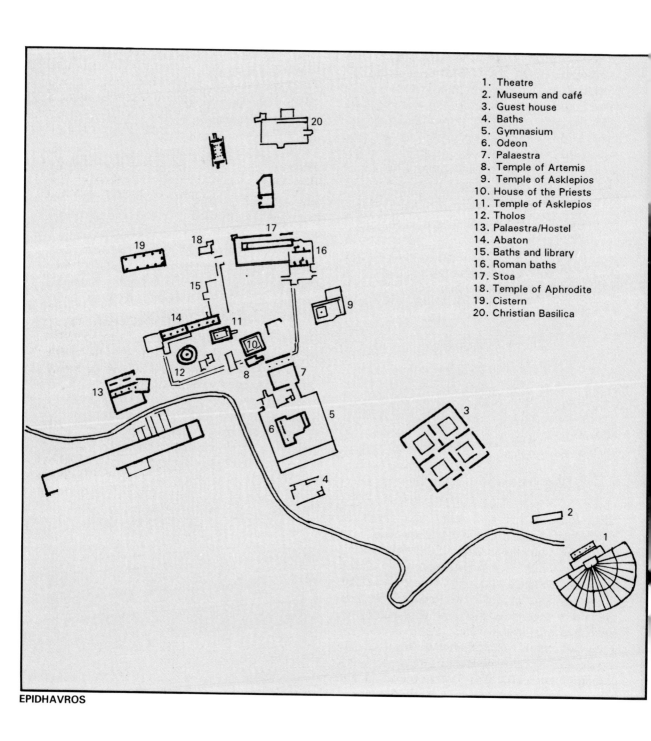

1. Theatre
2. Museum and café
3. Guest house
4. Baths
5. Gymnasium
6. Odeon
7. Palaestra
8. Temple of Artemis
9. Temple of Asklepios
10. House of the Priests
11. Temple of Asklepios
12. Tholos
13. Palaestra/Hostel
14. Abaton
15. Baths and library
16. Roman baths
17. Stoa
18. Temple of Aphrodite
19. Cistern
20. Christian Basilica

EPIDHAVROS

Epidhavros theatre. Test the accoustics for yourself - you can hear paper rustling or a coin dropped in the orchestra from the top row of seats.

One interesting point is that I have heard music buffs claim that modern (from the last500 years!) compositions played by orchestras here do not sound as they should - strings and woodwinds are distorted they say. This may be because the theatre was designed to throw the human voice and a few assorted percussion and string instruments to the audience and the sort of design needed for an open-air theatre to do that is different from the sort of auditorium needed for a modern orchestra.

You can get to Epidhavros from Palaia Epidhavros (around 12 kilometres) or from Navplion (around 30 kilometres). In the summer a theatre festival is staged putting on ancient Greek drama (albeit in Demotic Greek) and excursions are arranged from Palaia Epidhavros and Navplion. It is worth going for the spectacle under the night sky even if you don't understand the play though do take a cushion - those stone seats get awfully hard after an hour or two.

Kolpos Epidhavrou

From Palaia Epidhavros the Gulf of Epidhavros extends southeast enclosed by the coast of the Peloponnese on the west and the Methana peninsula on the east. There are several anchorages around the gulf that can be used in calm weather and the weather here is often settled in the summer with long periods of calm.

Lesia. A cove on the west side of the gulf off a small hamlet approximately 3 miles southeast of Ak Nisadha. Anchor in 2-10 metres tucked in as far as possible.

Psifti. In the southwest corner of the gulf. A few fishing boats are kept on rickety wooden jetties here.

Isthmus Bay. A bay in the southeast corner of the gulf on the west side of the isthmus connecting Methana peninsula to the Peloponnese. There is a small inlet immediately north which looks worth exploring.

Ormos Pounda. The large bay under Ak Pounda. Anchor in 3-8 metres in the northern corner. There are irregular rocky depths immediately off the shore. A good barbecue spot-weather permitting.

Methana Peninsula (Khersonisos Methana)

This triangular peninsula juts out from the coast of the Peloponnese connected only by a narrow isthmus at Taktikoupolis. Methana is as near perfect an example of the word peninsula (from the Latin *paene,* almost, and *insula,* island -the Greek Khersonisos means much the same) as you are going to get. Its origins are volcanic as even a cursory look at the jagged rubble strewn slopes will tell. The crater of the volcano is in the northwest corner of the peninsula near the village of Kaimeni (properly Kaimeni Khora-the "burnt village") and Strabo (63BC - AD21) recorded a violent eruption here although whether he in fact witnessed it is not known.

Ancient Methana was not where modern

Methana peninsula just north of Vathi.

Methana is today as some guide books erroneously assume, but was on the west coast south of Vathi. There are extensive ruins here, some of which have been used in the construction of a Byzantine castle, but to date no systematic excavation has been carried out. Pausanias in his 2nd century tour and commentary made the following observations on the volcanic nature of Methana.

"A little under four miles away there are hot springs; they say the water first appeared only when Antigonos was king in Macedonia: what appeared first was not water but fire blazing up above the earth, and when it died down the water sprang out. It still comes up hot nowadays and powerfully salty. But if you wash in it no cold water is available anywhere near, and if you dive into the sea the swimming is dangerous as there are numbers of marine monsters including sharks."
Pausanias *Guide To Greece* Vol 1 transl. Peter Levi.

This reference to an abundance of sharks where there are hot springs is interesting and one I have heard before, both from ancient commentators and modern locals. Off Isola di Vulcano in the Lipari Islands in Italy similar stories are told and at Bencik in the Gulf of Hisaronu in Turkey sharks are said to be abundant where warm springs well up into the sea. I can't say I have ever noticed sharks in any of these locations, Methana included, but it would make sense that sharks would breed where hot springs increased the sea temperature.

There are two harbours yachts can use on the peninsula and several anchorages depending on the weather. If you go walking on the peninsula take stout footwear, a hat and water - the volcanic rock seems to intensify the heat and its sharp surfaces are hard on shoes.

Vathi

A small fishing harbour on the west coast of the Methana peninsula.

Pilotage

Approach The exact location of the harbour is initially difficult to determine, especially from the northwest, but closer in the breakwater and the houses of the hamlet will be seen. The entrance is nearly impossible to make out until you are right up to it although a white mast on the south side of the entrance and the light structure on the end of the breakwater will be seen. Care is needed in the entrance which is very narrow and bordered by underwater rocks on both sides.

Vathi looking out from the slopes behind.

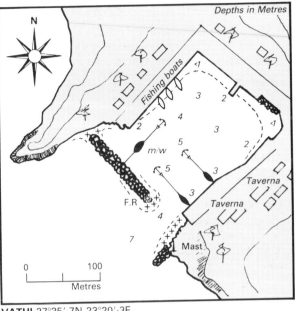

VATHI 37°35'·7N 23°20'·3E

Mooring Go stern or bows-to the quay on the south where there are good depths right up to the quay. The bottom is mud and weed and poor holding in patches. Good shelter from all winds now the new breakwater has been built.

Facilities

Water from the taverna. Several tavernas which often have fresh fish which will be simply grilled over charcoal as it should be in a place like this. Other tavernas on the beach at Paralia a short walk south. Some provisions available at Paralia. Taxi. Occasional bus to Methana town.

General

The hamlet is a delightfully peaceful spot and is only now becoming popular with yachts. Outside of August it is little visited. Much of the coast nearby is covered in pine on the lower slopes, especially north of the hamlet. The upper slopes are strewn with jagged volcanic rubble as is most of the peninsula.

Just south of the hamlet are the ruins of ancient Methana which received little more than a nod at its existence from ancient commentators. Pausanias mentioned a temple to Isis here, the Egyptian deity was Hellenized and then Romanized, and since the rituals dealt with fire and water it is perhaps not surprising the cult was introduced to this volcanic peninsula.

Chapel Cove

North of Vathi a small white chapel on Ak Krasopanayia is conspicuous. With care a yacht can anchor in here or in the adjacent cove in settled weather. With a strong *meltemi* there are little whirlwinds in here and it is best avoided. It is deep for anchoring so if stopping just for lunch use the kedge rather than the bower anchor. The coves are quite deserted under steep pine-clad slopes except for a few local fishermen who potter around here. The chapel (*Panayia Krasata*) was apparently built by a wine merchant saved from shipwreck near here and wine is said to have been used instead of water when the mortar was mixed.

Vathi looking from the north side across to the yacht quay

Paralia Kounoupitsa

On the northeast tip of the peninsula there is a small harbour that can be used with care in calm weather. A large church on the shore is conspicuous. Care is needed as the entrance is rockbound and the depths variable. There are depths of around 2 metres in the entrance and 1-1.5 metre depths inside. Alternatively anchor off the hamlet in calm weather. Taverna ashore.

The chapel on the northwest corner of Methana peninsula. In settled weather you can anchor in the cove under the point.

Methana

The main harbour and ferry port for the peninsula. The yacht harbour is south of the ferry pier behind a headland connected by a low isthmus to the peninsula.

Pilotage

Approach   The buildings of the town of Methana spread along the shore on the southeast side of the peninsula and are easily identified from the distance. The yacht harbour lies tucked away behind a headland to the south of the town and the entrance will not be seen from the north until you are around the headland. From the south the headland and entrance are easily identified. Care is needed in the narrow entrance which leaves little room for careless driving especially if someone is coming the other way.

Mooring   Go stern or bows-to the quay on the west side where convenient. There are shallow patches off the quay but it is all soft mud and you won't do any damage on it. The holding is good in the gluey black mud on the bottom, but when you haul the anchor up it deposits itself all over the boat and the crew and is damnably difficult to remove. Shelter in the harbour is all-round and numerous yachts are kept permanently here.

The harbour is classified as a marina and a charge is made, though not on the scale of the purpose-built marinas around Athens.

Facilities

Services Water on the quay. Electricity available. Fuel delivered by mini-tanker.

Provisions Good shopping for all provisions in the town. Ice available.

Eating Out Tavernas in the town, though none outstanding that I have tried.

Other Bank. PO. OTE. Ferries and hydrofoils to Aegina, Piraeus, Poros, and to Idhra and other destinations south.

General

The hydropathic institute and your nose tells you immediately that this was once a spa resort utilising the sulphurous warm water that bubbles out of the ground and the sea. Presumably these springs are those mentioned by Pausanias and it is off here that "marine monsters and sharks" were found. The village above the harbour is called Vromolimni which literally means "stinking shore", a further reference to the sulphurous springs. The springs are said to be beneficial to those suffering from rheumatism, arthritis, dermatological complaints and nervous disorders (is anyone excluded?) and boats kept in the harbour are said not to suffer from fouling problems.

With all this going for it you might think Methana would be a bright and breezy place, but perhaps the miasma rising over the town envelops any euphoria as most people find it a torpid and enervating spot and nobody really remembers much about the town except for the smell and the black mud in the harbour.

The narrow entrance into Methana harbour.

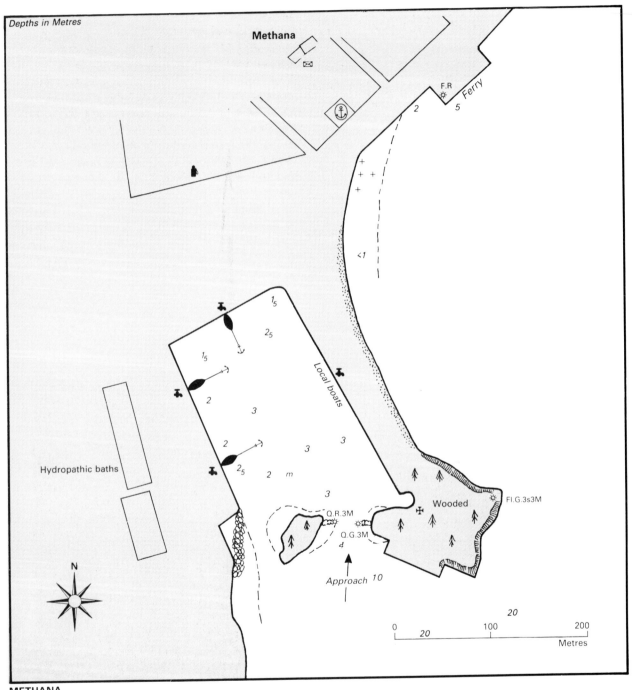

Depths in Metres

Methana

F.R

Ferry

2

5

Local boats

Hydropathic baths

Wooded

Fl.G.3s3M

Q.R.3M

Q.G.3M

4

Approach 10

N

20

0   20   100   200

Metres

METHANA
37°34'·6N 23°23'·5E (Fl.G.3s3M)

Nisos Aegina (Aiyina)

Aegina lying only 12 miles from Piraeus (though it is around 17 miles from Zea and 18 miles from Kalamaki to Aegina harbour) is a popular weekend destination for Athenians escaping the smog of Athens whether by yacht, ferry or hydrofoil. It is not uncommon in the summer to find a nautical traffic jam between the island and Piraeus as everyone hurtles towards the harbour intent on finding a berth. Outside August and the weekends it is a remarkably tranquil spot and surprisingly little developed for such a popular resort.

The island has had its ups and downs. Its mythopaeic origins are derived yet again from the satyriac activities of Zeus who bedded Aegina, loveliest of the daughters of the river Asopos. To hide his sexual activities from his wife Zeus transported her to the island of Oinone which then became Aegina. I haven't counted the number of times poor old Zeus transported his loves out of the sight and wrath of Hera, but it is a recurring theme. Aegina gave birth on the island to Zeus' son Aiakos who though not well known in the pantheon of the gods, had two sons, Peleus and Telamon, who in turn sired Achilles (he of the vulnerable heel) and Ajax (courageous but a bit stupid).

From excavations at Kolona to the north of modern Aegina town numerous Neolithic remains have been found and occupation of this site continued through the Bronze Age. There are several Mycenean sites around the island indicating that it was important during this period and indeed Homer records that Aegina

The chapel at the entrance to Aegina harbour.

sent a fleet of 80 ships to Troy. The real period of prosperity for the island began in the 7th century BC and by the 6th century Aegina had established trading posts around the Aegean and up into the Black Sea and down to the Nile. It even minted its own coins with the image of a turtle on them, one of the first Greek city-states to do, and established courts of law and even an embryonic state health system.

It was inevitable that the proximity of Aegina to Athens would arouse the wrath of the Athenians and so it did. Athens had difficulty persuading Aegina to send thirty ships to Salamis to fight with the Athenian fleet against the Persians, but it was a near run thing as Aegina did not want to antagonise their trading partners in the east. As it was the ships from Aegina proved critical and distinguished themselves above the others in the battle.

After Salamis relationships between the two city-states deteriorated again - Pericles in Aristotle's *Rhetoric* demanded that the Athenians rid themselves of this "sore spot in the eye of Piraeus" - and in 458 BC Athens invaded the island, destroyed the city walls, confiscated most of the fleet and forced Aegina to join the Delian League. During the Peloponnesian war Aegina escaped from the Athenian yoke by siding with Sparta. Athens responded by expelling the population and the island never recovered.

It declined in importance during the Roman period and in the ninth century AD the capital was moved from the port to Palaiochora after repeated pirate attacks. Not until 1827 did it become prominent again when it became the first capital of newly freed Greece. The first modern Greek coins were minted here (a nice synchronicity with the 6th century BC) in 1829 though in the same year the capital was moved to Navplion. In recent years its proximity to Athens has aroused not envy but a thankfulness that there is somewhere away from the hubbub and pollution of the city to escape to.

Getting Around

Motorbikes and bicycles can be hired in Aegina town and this is the logical place from which to explore inland. Bicycles are probably best left for the cooler months if you are going any distance. The road system on the island is basically a ring road around the island (though the last stretch between Portes and Perdika is not yet completed) and a road across the middle of the island from Aegina town to Aghia Marina.

It is well worth visiting Palaiochora in the middle of the island where the inhabitants retreated to in the Middle Ages. There are only the ruins of the houses left, but all the churches (twenty five of them) are intact and in good repair although sadly not all the murals inside are - an attendant is normally on the site most mornings. Further on from Palaiochora stands the Temple to Aphaia on a wooded outcrop looking over Aghia Marina.

Aegina harbour. *Nigel Patten.*

Limin Aegina

The main ferry port and capital situated on the west side of the island.

Pilotage

Approach From Athens the harbour will not be seen until you round Ak Plakakia though houses spread from the town right up to the cape. The light structure on the cape is easily recognised and there are usually numerous hydrofoils heading towards or from the cape. From the northwest the town is easily identified and from the south it will be seen once you are past Nisis Moni. Closer in the single Doric column standing on Ak Kolona immediately north of the harbour will be seen and the harbour breakwaters and entrance are easily identified.

Care needs to be taken of the shoal water extending from the harbour across to Nisos Anghistri and of the shallows and reefs either side of Nisis Metopi. The shallows are only really a danger if you are coming from the west or headed from Aegina to Anghistri. However from the south or when heading south from the harbour do not stray too close to Nisis Metopi. Close to the entrance a red buoy marks a 2.5 metre rock and the buoy can be left to port or starboard.

In the immediate approaches care is needed of the car ferries and hydrofoils using the harbour and they should be given right of way in this bottleneck boat-jam.

The approach to Aegina harbour looking north.

Mooring Go stern or bows-to the town quay. In the summer the quay gets very crowded. When the "marina" immediately south of the harbour is finished the number of yachts that can be accommodated here will be considerably increased. The bottom in the harbour and the "marina" is mud and weed, poor holding in places so make sure your anchor is well in. Good shelter in the harbour from the *meltemi* but westerlies cause a surge, more uncomfortable than dangerous, and southerlies send in a swell which with a strong blow can be very uncomfortable and possibly dangerous.

Note The small "marina" under construction on the south side of the harbour was well advanced at the time of writing with the outer breakwater complete and ready for the T-piers to be installed. Ancillary facilities will probably take longer to be completed. It is likely that it will be in operation in 1993.

Facilities

Services Water can be delivered by mini-tanker. Fuel near the quay and a mini-tanker will deliver.

Provisions Good shopping for provisions in the town. Several *caiques* on the town quay sell fruit and vegetables. Ice available from the fish market near the quay.

Eating Out Good tavernas on the waterfront and even better ones behind. One street back from the quay is *Vostanios* serving good Greek fare. On the west side of the town is the "Chicken Shop" serving spit-roast chicken and pork which is good value. Behind the market is an *ouzerie* which has good grilled octopus.

Other Bank. PO. OTE. Hire motorbikes and bicycles. Ferries and hydrofoils to Piraeus and south to Methana, Poros, Idhra and other destinations south.

General

The difficult approaches to the harbour were well known and commented on by Pausanias though he goes a bit too far in his caution.

"Aegina is the most unapproachable island in Greece, there are rocks underwater or just

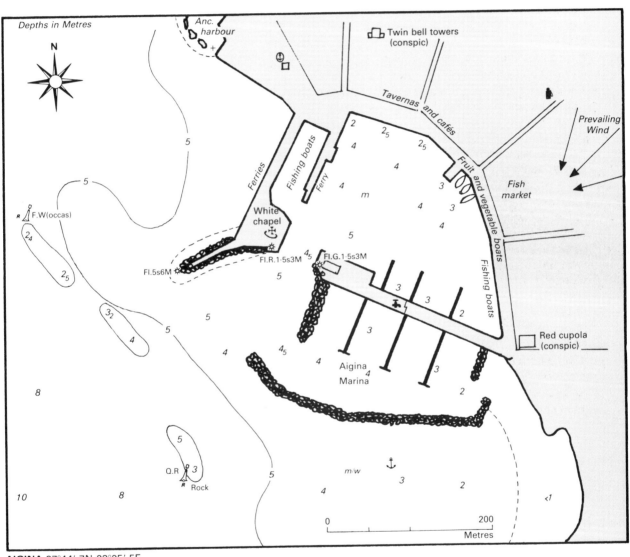

Depths in Metres

N

Anc. harbour

Twin bell towers (conspic)

Tavernas and cafés

Prevailing Wind

Ferries

Fishing boats

Ferry

Fruit and vegetable boats

Fish market

5

5

R F.W(occas)

White chapel

2₄

2₅

m

5

Fl.5s6M

Fl.R.1·5s3M

4₅

Fl.G.1·5s3M

3₂

4

5

5

5

4₅

4₅

3

3

Fishing boats

Aigina Marina

Red cupola (conspic)

8

4

2

Q.R

5

3

Rock

R

m/w

3

2

10

8

4

<1

0   200
Metres

AIGINA 37°44'·7N 23°25'·5E

Aegina harbour

years with prosperous merchants houses - fortunately the 19th century core of the town has altered little since.

On the flat plain south of Aegina town there are numerous stands of pistachio trees which were introduced to the island on a commercial basis in the early 20th century to boost the flagging agricultural economy and now Aegina pistachios (*fistikia Aeginis*- literally peanuts of Aegina) are known all over the Aegean. They are on sale everywhere in the town.

Souvalas

A small harbour situated approximately midway along the north coast. Reasonable shelter can be found tucked behind the mole if there is room amongst the local boats. Go bows-to the outer end of the mole where there are mostly 2 metre depths. Further into the harbour depths are irregular and shallower. Keep well clear of the pier on the south side where the landing-craft type ferry berths. Reasonable shelter from the *meltemi* although with strong northerlies there is a surge in the harbour.

breaking the surface all around it. They say Aiakos contrived it like this deliberately, for fear of sea pirates and to make it dangerous to enemies".

Pausanias *Guide To Greece Vol.1* transl. Peter Levi

In fact the approach was more dangerous in ancient times when there were two harbours, the present one (much rebuilt) which was the commercial harbour and the military harbour northwest of the present harbour which was reputed to have a secret entrance between the rocks known only to trusted Aeginites.

The present town is largely a result of its elevation as capital of the infant Greece in 1827 when most of the prominent buildings were planned and constructed. Although the capital was transferred to Navplion in 1829 the prominent public buildings and the grid layout of the town remained and were added to in later

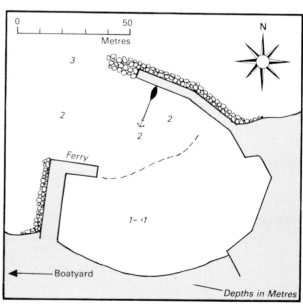

SOUVALAS

Tavernas ashore. To the west of the harbour there are several boatyards.

There are hot springs nearby said to be beneficial for the usual range of ailments, rheumatism, arthritis and so on, but most of the population seem to be here not for the spa but for the clear air and commute to Athens in the summer.

Aghia Marina

The large bay on the east side of the island. A large hotel and several smaller buildings around the bay are conspicuous. The anchorage in the bay is not the best with northerlies and is untenable with a healthy *meltemi* blowing. It is also open south so is only really tenable in calm weather or westerlies. Anchor in the northwest of the bay in 4-10 metres on sand, rocks and weed, not everywhere the best holding. Do not go onto the piers off the shore which are for tripper boats bringing visitors to the bay and the temple.

If the weather is not suitable for a stop here a yacht can always go to Aegina town and visit the temple by bus or taxi. Several tavernas on the beach and at the temple site.

The Temple of Aphaia deserves a visit for its elegant simplicity and for its position in the mysterious temple triangle. It is dedicated to Aphaia, a Cretan deity popular in Mycenean times, whose cult was later dedicated to Athena. It was built on the site of a more ancient temple in 490 BC and thus predates the Parthenon by a few years. The style of the temple is Doric and 24 of the original 32 columns are standing after being re-erected in 1960.

This temple completes the almost perfect isosceles triangle that can be drawn between the Parthenon, the temple on Sounion, and here. The mystery is a real one since the initial construction of a temple on Sounion was interrupted by the Persians in 490 BC (the present temple on Sounion dates from 444 BC) as was the construction of the Temple of Aphaia. The Parthenon was begun in 447 BC so it ties in with the later completion dates of the other two temples. Thus all three temples are of the same era but is it likely they would describe a perfect isosceles triangle by coincidence or was the geometry of the ancient Greeks more sophisticated than we credit them for - a small isosceles triangle is one thing but one with sides 24 miles long is another.

Southern Anchorages

Around the south end of the island there are several anchorages that can be used in calm weather or light northerlies.

Ormos Kipos. Lies under Ak Andonis. Care is needed of above and below water rocks fringing the coast. Anchor in 4-10 metres where convenient.

Ormos Pirgos. Lies immediately west of Ak Pirgos. Anchor in 4-10 metres.

Kato Perdika. A bay immediately south of Perdika. Anchor off in 5-10 metres on sand and weed.

Ormos Pirgos on the southern end of Aegina. *Nigel Patten.*

Perdika

A small fishing village and resort on the southeast of Aegina. There is little room in here for yachts so you will have to squeeze in where you can.

Pilotage

Approach   The hamlet and inlet are not easily seen from the north or south until you are up to the entrance. However the location is obvious opposite Nisis Moni.

Mooring   Go stern or bows-to either side of the inside short pier if there is room or anchor off in the southeast corner taking care of the shallows. Leave the end of the pier clear for the water boat which comes alongside. If possible it is best to be on the pier where it is more comfortable. The outer mole is taken up

PERDIKA
37°41′N 23°27′E

The inner mole at Perdika. Leave room for the water-boat on the end.

with permanent berths. The bottom is mud and weed, patchy holding in parts. Good shelter from all but strong westerlies.

Facilities

Water on the quay. Provisions available ashore. Numerous tavernas along the waterfront several of which usually have locally caught fish. The taverna immediately above the pier or the prosaically named *No 10* are as good as any.

General

Perdika was once a small fishing village but it is now about fifty-fifty resort and fishing village. It retains a pleasant shambolic sort of charm with the houses seemingly piled on top of one another along the waterfront. There always seems to be something going on here - boats chugging in and out, wives yelling at husbands not to stay too long at the taverna, and tourists on the waterfront watching it all.

Perdika means "partridge" and although there don't seem many around these days, they were once a pest and were culled annually to prevent them eating the corn growing on the island. George Wheeler gives us this description from the time of the Turkish occupation.

"Aegina hath great plenty of corn, cotton, honey and wax; also abundance of almonds, and *keratia,* or carobs. It abounds also with a sort of red-legged partridges, that by order of the epitropi, or the chief magistrates of the town, all, both young and old, women and children, go out yearly, as the pygmies of old did against the cranes, to war with them, and to break their eggs before they be hatch'd; otherwise, by their multitudes, they would so destroy, and eat up the corn, that they would inevitably bring a famine every year upon the place. But they say, there are no hares at all in this island."

George Wheeler *Journey Into Greece 1682*

Perdika.

Nisis Moni

The island immediately opposite Perdika. It is conspicuous in the southern approaches to Aegina and when heading south from Aegina town. The passage between the island and Aegina is deep and free of dangers in the fairway.

On the north side of the island yachts can anchor off the camping ground ashore. Here there is good shelter from southerlies. A taverna opens in the summer.

On the southeast side of the island there is a cove surrounded by cliffs that can be used in calm weather. It is very deep and you will need to take a line ashore to the north side. The bottom is strewn with boulders so use a trip-line on the anchor.

The island is called Moni simply because it was once owned by the Monastery of Chrysoleontissa in the middle of Aegina. It is now owned by the Touring Club of Greece who run the camping ground set amongst the pine trees. There are said to be numbers of peacocks on the island.

The anchorage tucked under the southeast side of Moni. In calm weather only.

Nisis Petrokaravo and Nisis Platia

South of Aegina are two small islets lying in the sea area between Aegina and Poros. Nisis Petrokaravo is a line of high jagged rocks, easily identified and looking something like their name - the "stone ship". Nisis Platia is a low flat islet less easily identified.

Petrokaravo, the line of jagged rocks between Aegina and Poros.

Nisos Anghistri

Anghistri sits just 3½ miles from Aegina town connected to it by shoal water and indeed sometime in the past Aegina and Anghistri must have been one island. Despite its proximity to Aegina and to Athens it is little visited by tourists or for that matter by yachts.

The main town and capital is Milo (or Megalokhorio or Anghistri) on the north of the island. The small port for the island is Skala (or Metokhi) on the northeast. The only other settlement of any size is at Limenaria in the south and naturally enough the only roads on the island are between these three settlements. Much of the island is wooded in pine and there are some good walks through the interior and around the coast.

Little is known about Anghistri in ancient times. It was called Kekryfalia and may have had some association with Kekrops, the mythical first ruler of Athens who is often depicted as being a serpent from the waist down, though this may simply be a vague relegation of the island to the mists of time as it were, a position it still holds if you listen to Aeginites talking about the backwardness of the islanders Much of the present population are said to be of Albanian extraction, but I often find this is simply a pseudonym for Greeks who are not from Attica.

Skala Anghistri

Pilotage

Approach   The buildings around the harbour are easily identified but care is needed in the approaches because of the reefs and shallows extending eastwards from this corner of the island. The approach is best made from the southeast so that you avoid the stretch of shoal water. From the north it is possible to enter through Stenon Anghistri between Nisis Metopi and Anghistri though considerable care is needed. There are least depths of 5 metres in the fairway.

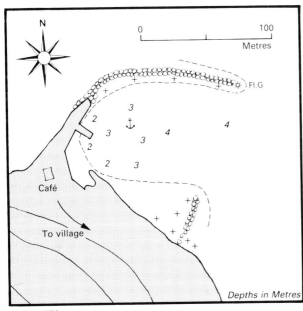

ANGISTRI
37°43′N 23°21′E

Mooring   Moor bows to the outer end of the quayed area if there is room or anchor off with a long-line to the breakwater. Keep well clear of the ferry berths and the area where the ferries must manoeuvre. With a strong *meltemi* the harbour is very uncomfortable and with strong southerlies untenable. Use in settled conditions with light northeasterlies or southeasterlies.

Facilities

Basic provisions can be found here and there are numerous tavernas in the summer. Ferry to Aegina.

General

Skala is a comparatively modern place compared to the other settlements on the island and it is well worth taking the small island bus to Milo. Here the narrow streets and old houses on the waters edge make it an enchanting and friendly place.

Limenaria

A small fishing village on the southeast side of the island. The cove off the village is nothing more than a cleft in the cliffs but just northeast there is a shallow patch which can be used in calm weather only.

Nisis Dhorousa Anchorages

On the southwest tip of the island opposite Nisis Dhorousa are several bays affording better shelter than might be evident from the chart. The channel between Nisis Dhorousa and Anghistri is deep and free of dangers in the fairway. The slopes around here are thickly wooded in pine and it is an idyllic spot that can be reached only by water. The southerly of the bays is the most popular and is well sheltered from the prevailing winds (NE and SE) and as a bonus a taverna opens in the summer.

Skala Anghistri. *Nigel Patten*

Nisos Poros

Poros means a "strait" or a "crossing", a name that fits perfectly once you have seen the approaches to Poros town. At its narrowest, off the town proper, the island is separated by a mere 300 metres or so from the mainland and much of this is shallow so that the navigable channel is only a 100 metres wide. Pausanias described how you could walk right across in the 2nd century AD though he didn't say if he tried it. The approach to the town from the sea is one of the most attractive in Greece and Henry Miller provides one of the best descriptions in his classic *The Colossus of Maroussi.*

"... suddenly I realised we were sailing through the streets. If there is one dream which I like above all others it is that of sailing on land. Coming into Poros gives the illusion of a deep dream. Suddenly the land converges on all sides and the boat is squeezed into a narrow strait from which there appears to be no egress. The men and women in Poros are hanging out of the windows, just above your head. You pull in right under their friendly nostrils, as though for a shave and a haircut en route. The loungers on the quay are walking with the same speed as the boat; they can walk faster than the boat if they chose to quicken their pace."

Never mind that ferries and hydrofoils speed in and out of the strait, that landing-craft ferries churn across to Galatas, that bars compete for the highest decibel level and the most banal offerings, that villas now spread out like a canker from the old town and sub-divisions indicate there will be more, never mind all that because the essence of Miller's description is there and those of us who have spent some time here have a fondness for the place that eclipses

Poros looking from the rocky ridge above the town ..."Suddenly the land converges on all sides". *Photo Nigel Patten*

all this and endorses his words. And it has something else other than the appearance of a little Greek Venice, it has a sensuality, a calm (especially during siesta time), and what can only be described as a conviviality despite the fact that the constant coming and going of ferries and hydrofoils makes life a misery for yachts on the quay.

Poros is composed of two islands today joined by a narrow isthmus which were described separately in ancient times. The small island on which the present day town stands was called Sphaeria and the larger island Kalauria or Kalavria which means "good breeze", a reference to the mild and comparatively gentle version of the *meltemi* which blows across the island. Today this version of the *meltemi* which tends to blow in from the east-northeast is called the *boukadhoura*. Ancient Kalauria was built above the bay of Ormos Barbaria or Vagyonias on the north of the island though

little remains today except the foundations of the Temple to Poseidon.

The temple was well known as a sanctuary in ancient times and it was here that Demosthenes (384-322BC), arguably the greatest orator in Athens, sought safety after his politics could no longer be tolerated. To save his honour he committed suicide with poison concealed in the quill of his pen. Ancient Kaularia must have been of some importance as it was the headquarters of the Kaularian League of the 7th century BC, a fairly loose association between Kaularia, Troezen on the mainland and Aegina designed to keep pirates at bay.

Nothing much of historical note occurred here until the 19th century when the island became involved along with Idhra and Spetsai in the Greek Revolution against the Turks. The Greek fleet and foreign sympathisers used the sheltered anchorage off Poros as the fleet anchorage to regroup and take on supplies.

Poros looking from the east end of the narrow channel

Towards the end of the revolution old enmities began to surface and when Capodistrias, President of the Assembly, secretly signed an edict that would effectively end the brigandage the Idhriots had traditionally occupied themselves with, trouble was brewing. The edict specifically detailed a blockade of the Port of Idhra and measures to prevent boats without valid documents from sailing, which it was hoped would control the endemic piracy. It should be remembered that the fleets from Idhra and Spetsai were as inclined to attack British, French or Russian ships (their ostensible allies) for booty as they were to attack Turkish or Egyptian ships for the cause of the revolution - and the spoils of war.

The admiral of the Greek fleet, Miaoulis, an Idhriot and former brigand, upon learning of the edict immediately set sail with his ships to Poros and captured the largest ship of the Greek fleet, the frigate *Hellas*, and the fort on Aghios Konstandinos. The Russian navy was brought in to deal with the rebel admiral and Miaoulis, faced by superior forces, decided to blow up the *Hellas* and several other ships. The act was universally condemned, even by Idhriots. As if to forestall any further rebellion the main navy dockyard was installed at Poros until it was moved to Salamis in 1881. A naval college still remains and for many years the old coal-burning dreadnought *Averoff* was berthed off here until its removal, much to the anger of the locals, to Faliron.

Today Poros is a popular resort for Athenians and foreigners alike. Nearly all of this attraction is centred on Poros town or the nearby coast and for the most part the island is rugged and unpopulated. The only roads on the island run west to Russian Bay, east to the monastery of Zoodochos Pigi, or around a circular route via the Temple of Poseidon in the middle of the island. On the opposite shore Galatas is a more down-to-earth less touristy place serving the agricultural hinterland. The area is well known for its extensive citrus groves which spread out to the west from the village and is known locally as *limonodassus*, "the lemon forest".

The approach to Poros town looking east.

Getting around

Given the limited road system it is questionable whether it is worth hiring a motorbike or car, yet they are available at Poros town. Hire bicycles are also available and these would seem to make more sense. *Caique* ferries run everywhere as far as Russian Bay and Monastery Bay and of course across to Galatas. At Galatas it is possible to hire motorbikes and the obvious place to make for would be ancient Troezen and the Devil's Gorge to the west of Galatas.

Limin Poros

The main harbour for the island lies tucked away in the strait between the island and the Peloponnese. Neither entrance into the strait is obvious from the distance although the ferries and hydrofoils apparently disappearing and appearing from the land in the summer gives a clue to the whereabouts of the entrances.

Pilotage

Approach　From the north head past Methana town towards the slit in the low cliffs that will just be discerned. Closer in the small lighthouse on Ak Dana and the light structure on Ak Nedha will be seen. Once around Ak Nedha, Poros town will be seen and the approach is obvious. Care is needed of ferries and hydrofoils leaving Poros as they

cannot be seen until you are around Ak Nedha when you will encounter them heading for the channel at full speed which means 32 knots in the case of hydrofoils.

From the southeast it is difficult to see the entrance and the low land of the isthmus between Sphaeria and Kalauria is sometimes mistaken for the entrance. Nisis Bourtzi with a fort on it is easily identified and closer in the light structure will be seen. Once around the corner you are literally in the harbour. Like the north entrance care is needed of ferries and hydrofoils leaving the harbour and also arriving - don't forget to look over your shoulder occasionally.

Once into the narrow strait between the town quay and Galatas care is needed of the shallow mud bank extending out from the southwest side of the channel. It is not marked and can be difficult to see if the numbers of yachts going aground in the summer is anything to go by.

Mooring　Yachts berth either alongside or stern or bows-to the town quay just east of the ferry quay. Chunks of the quay are reserved for the ferries and hydrofoils, *caique* ferries to Galatas, fishing boats, and a number of charter companies. There can sometimes be a current in the channel of up to 1-1½ knots, usually in the direction the wind has been blowing. Yachts also berth stern or bows-to the north quay. The bottom in the channel is soft　mud　and　off　the　north

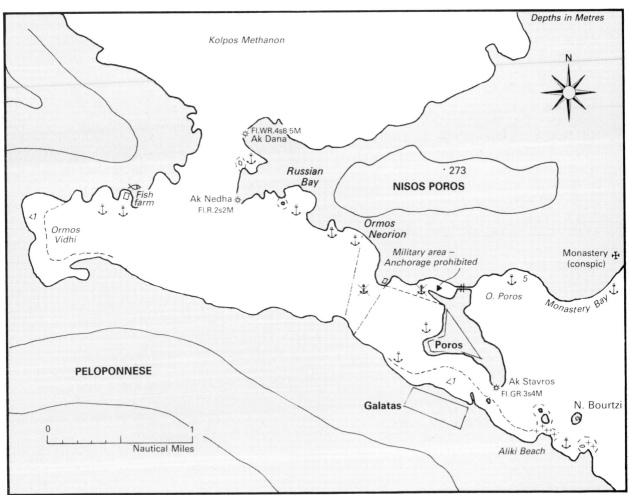

Depths in Metres

Kolpos Methanon

Fl.WR.4s8.5M
Ak Dana

Russian
Bay

NISOS POROS

· 273

Fish
farm

Ak Nedha
Fl.R.2s2M

Ormos
Neorion

Monastery
(conspic)

<1

Ormos
Vidhi

Military area –
Anchorage prohibited

O. Poros

5

Monastery Bay

Poros

PELOPONNESE

Ak Stavros
Fl.GR.3s4M

N. Bourtzi

Galatas

<1

0   1
Nautical Miles

Aliki Beach

APPROACHES TO POROS

quay mud and weed, not always the best holding in the latter. Shelter in the channel is excellent. Shelter on the north quay is good in the summer (the *meltemi* does not blow home) and in spring and autumn unless a strong northwesterly blows down off the hills.

The biggest problem in Poros is usually not the wind but the wash from the ferries and hydrofoils. If you are alongside in the channel the boat can be damaged unless you pay attention to warps and fenders - make sure you put springs on. Even stern or bows-to in the channel or on the north quay you will be rocked around by ferry wash and inconsiderate motorboats and small ferries speeding around so make sure your anchor is properly in and

Poros looking from the channel.

85

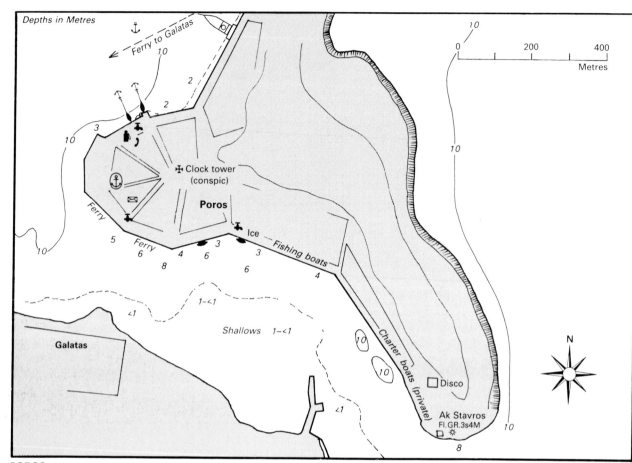

POROS
37°30′N 23°27′E

you are pulled well off the quay. It can also get a bit smelly in the channel in the hot summer months.

Facilities

Services Water on the north quay and by arrangement with a bar or taverna in the channel. Fuel delivered by mini-tanker. Showers available in some of the bars.

Provisions Good shopping for all provisions around the waterfront. Ice available from some bars.

Eating Out Numerous tavernas of all types and persuasion on the waterfront. If you climb up to the square on the slopes above you will find *Dhrougas,* locally known as

"the garage" for obvious reasons when you see it, which serves honest Greek fare and good home-made *retsina*. In Galatas right at the southeast end of the village is *Vlachos* which though it doesn't have a very inspiring view over the local football field, does have excellent Greek food and good local wine. On the quay *Sotiros* has an interesting and above average selection and entertainment from the host who is let us say eccentric in his mannerisms. I suggest you avoid anywhere that has "brother" in the title or anywhere that touts - the good tavernas in Poros don't need to have someone directing you to a seat. On the waterfront Yiorgios at the *Cafe Remezzo* serves a good breakfast and is something of a

The 'sleeping lady' behind Poros. It is best viewed at sunset as here.

local for yachties here. The *Monkey Bar* also serves as something of a local.

Other . Banks. PO. OTE. Doctor and dentist. Laundrette on the north quay. Hire cars, motorbikes and bicycles. Ferries and hydrofoils north to Methana, Aegina, and Piraeus and south to Idhra, Ermioni, Spetsai and other destinations south.

General

I wonder how I can say that despite the wash from the ferries and hydrofoils, despite the competition for quay space, despite loud music from some of the bars, despite the day-trippers that pour in every day, Poros emerges through it all as a convivial and intimate place that many end up staying longer at than intended. It is a picturesque spot and I know people who have lived and worked here for years stand and watch the sun go down over the "sleeping lady" with a dreamy expression in their eyes.

The "sleeping lady" is the shape picked out of the hills in the west by the setting sun and unlike many similar epithets, the shape of the hills really does take on the appearance of a sleeping lady complete with most anatomical detail - it is best seen from the south end of the channel looking to the northwest. In a way it is the paradox of the place that gets to you, a picture postcard spot plagued by its very charm, a sort of Brighton-by-Aegean, that somehow retains its charm and you can't really figure out why.

The home of Greek Sails in Poros

Anchorages around Poros

There are numerous anchorages to the west and east of Poros town that can be used in settled weather or as an overnight anchorage.

Ormos Vidhi. The large bay on the east of Limin Porou. Anchor off the hamlet of Vidhi or in any of the coves on the north. The easternmost cove on the north has a fish farm in it but there is still room to anchor. The bottom here is mud and weed, good holding once you are through the weed though this can take some doing.

It is assumed the ancient port of Pogon, the harbour for Troezen, was situated here. The Athenian fleet gathered here before the Battle of Salamis and it was to here the women and children of Athens were evacuated before the battle.

Ak Dana anchorage. The cove immediately under Ak Dana affords good shelter from the prevailing winds and is comparatively free from ferry wash. Clear translucent water for swimming in.

Russian Bay. The first bay on the north side once into Limin Porou. It is easily recognised by the small islet in the middle with a white chapel on it. Anchor where convenient in 5-12 metre depths on mud and weed and take a long line ashore. Good shelter from the prevailing winds.

The bay is so named from the War of Independence when the Russian fleet was based here. The small chapel on the islet is called Thaskalio and is dedicated to teachers.

Ormos Neorion. The large bay to the east of Russian Bay. Anchor in 5-12 metres on mud and weed, good holding once through the weed. The best place to be is in the cove under the Villa Galini with a long line ashore. Good shelter from the prevailing winds. Care is needed of the two ski/parascending platforms in the bay. Hotels and taverna/bars ashore.

The Villa Galini on the edge of the bay is where Henry Miller and George Seferis spent some time, Miller writing his *The Colossus of Maroussi* and Seferis composing his poetry. Looking out from the villa Seferis wrote these words in his diary which capture still moments not just of Poros but of the Greek seascape.

"The sea was not beating, breathless. The pinetree needles were motionless like thorns of sea urchins at the depth of clear water. A black ship dragged along the line of the horizon little by little, like the cloth of the Karaghiozis theatre, underlined this amazing vision and disappeared."

Ormos Neorion. The anchorage under the Villa Galini.

Navy Bay. The bay immediately west of Poros town. It is prohibited to anchor in the north part off the naval college though the prohibition seems to be breached more and more each year. Anchor off the town quay in 10-16 metres.

Ormos Aliki. The bay tucked in between Nisis Bourtzi and Ak Aliki. Care needs to be taken not to cut across between Nisis Lazareto and the coast as a reef just under the water connects the two. Entrance can be made between Lazareto and Bourtzi or Bourtzi and Ak Aliki. Anchor in 3-10 metres. Good shelter from the prevailing winds. Taverna/bar and watersports centre ashore.

Ormos Askeli. The large bay between Sphaeria and Kalauria. Anchor off the north side in 5-15 metres on mud and weed, patchy holding in places. Good shelter from the prevailing wind. Taverna/bar ashore.

Monastery Bay. The bay under the monastery of Zoodhokos Pigi. A large and spectacularly uninspired hotel is conspicuous on the west of the bay. Anchor in 5-10 metres on the northeast side of the bay. Taverna/bar ashore.

The monastery of Zoodhokos Pigi (Virgin of the Life-giving Spring) above can be visited just a short climb above the anchorage. The monastery has a spring outside and the water is said to have curative properties.

Squiggle Bay. A bay on the northeast coast. In calm weather it is an idyllic spot but normally a swell is pushed in by the prevailing northeast-to-east wind. There are coves to the west and east which can also be used.

Ormos Barbaria (Vagyonias). The next large bay northwest of Squiggle Bay. Like the latter a swell is normally pushed into here but in calm weather it is an idyllic spot with a beach at the head of the bay. This is assumed to be the ancient harbour of Kaularia. Perhaps it was later used by invaders from the north or pirates and hence acquired the name Barbaria(n) - literally a non-Greek.

Ormos Ay Paraskevi. The bay to the northwest of Barbaria with the islet of Bisti in the entrance. The bay is very deep and also has a considerable swell pushed into it. With care you can anchor off the west side of Bisti in calm weather.

Ormos Voriarnia. An inlet on the west side of Poros. It is fringed by above and below water rocks so care is needed. A swell is normally pushed into here by the prevailing winds.

Caique converted for cruising in Ormos Neorion.

Troezen

Near the village of Dhamalas approximately 10 kilometres from Galatas are the ruins of ancient Troezen. The city was an important one in antiquity, one of the Kaularian League and the city to which Athens evacuated the women and children before the Battle of Salamis.

Most of the ruins have been picked over for subsequent building work right up to the 20th century - it being much easier to collect ready-cut rock than to have to quarry it. Consequently the churches and other buildings nearby have much ancient masonry incorporated into them, a palimpsest of stone spanning the centuries. The chance recovery of the "Troezen Stone" recording Themistocles decree for the evacuation of Athens (see the section on the Battle of Salamis in the Introduction) was doing sterling service as a doorstep at the local school until identified.

Troezen was established in the 5th century BC and probably earlier. It was known as the birthplace of Theseus, he who killed the Minotaur and unceremoniously dumped Ariadne on Naxos. It was at Troezen that Theseus was told to move a heavy rock under which he would find the sword and sandals left for him by Aegeus and sure enough there is a rock here which has inevitably been dubbed Theseus' Rock - how do they find them? The town declined when it sided with Sparta in the Peloponnesian Wars and was subsequently sacked by Athens.

Enough of the foundations remain to make a visit interesting and there is the added benefit of the Devil's Bridge nearby. Here a stream rushes down a low ravine shaded by plane trees in a scene somehow more redolent of Scandinavia than of the Devil's work. The water is deliciously cool and it is a pleasant place to sit around and cool your feet in after walking around in the heat.

CHAPTER 3

IDHRA TO SPETSAI

And The Adjacent Coast

	Shelter	Mooring	Fuel	Water	Provisions	Tavernas	Plan
Tselevinia	C	C	O	O	O	O	
Nisis Soupia	C	C	O	O	O	O	
Ormos Dardiza	O	C	O	O	O	O	
Ermioni	A	AC	B	A	B	B	▪
Ormos Kapari	C	C	O	O	O	O	
Idhra							
Idhra harbour	B	A	B	A	O	A	▪
Mandraki	C	C	O	O	O	C	▪
Ormos Molos	C	C	O	O	O	O	
Petassi	O	C	O	O	O	O	
Ormos Ay Nikolaos	O	C	O	O	O	O	
Dhokos							
Dhokos cove	B	C	O	O	O	O	▪
Ormos Skindos	C	C	O	O	O	O	▪
Ormos Kranidhiou	C	C	O	O	O	O	
Ormos Metokhi	C	C	O	O	O	O	
Ormos Kosta	O	C	O	O	O	O	
Nisis Khinitsa	B	C	O	O	O	O	▪
Porto Kheli	A	AC	B	B	B	B	▪
West bay	B	C	O	O	O	O	▪
Light structure cove	C	C	O	O	O	O	▪
Kiln Bay	C	C	O	O	O	O	
Headland Bay	B	C	O	O	O	O	

	Shelter	Mooring	Fuel	Water	Provisions	Tavernas	Plan
Spetsai							
Baltiza	A	AC	A	A	B	A	▪
Dapia	C	AC	O	O	B	A	▪
Ormos Zoyioryia	B	C	O	O	O	C	
Ormos Ay Paraskevi	O	C	O	O	O	O	
Ormos Ay Anaryiroi	O	C	O	O	O	C	

South quay at Ermioni.

Porto Kheli.

This chapter covers Kolpos Idhras (the Gulf of Hydra) to the island of Spetsai and the nearby coast. Unlike the areas covered in the two previous chapters there are few ancient associations - I can hear sighs of relief already from those numbed by trying to make sense of scattered ancient masonry. There are more recent associations with the Greek War of Independence but we will come to that in due course.

Around Kolpos Idhras the mountains rise steeply from the sea on the Peloponnese side and equally so around the coast of Idhra. For the most part the mountains are barren rocky places except for a few places on the Peloponnese coast where startling patches of green betray an underwater spring. The islands of Idhra and Dhokos give the appearance of utter barrenness though on closer inspection the southwest end of Idhra is clothed in pine on the lower slopes and I am assured by the locals there is a patch or two inland where things can be grown. To the west the geography of the coast descends to more gentle outlines around Porto Kheli and Spetsai likewise has a gentle aspect of rolling hills rather than craggy mountains.

Prevailing Winds

The east-northeast winds blowing down onto Poros blow down to Nisidhes Tselevinia where they bend to blow from the east into Kolpos Idhras. With strong northeasterlies gusts blow off the high land on the coast. Around Nisos Dhokos the winds are usually variable and may be from the east or the southeast. Across to Spetsai winds are normally from the southeast in the summer though northeasterlies may extend as far as Spetsai.

The coast from Tselevinia to Ak Mouzaki

Nisidhes Tselevinia

These two islands, Nisis Skilli and Nisis Spathi lie 4½ miles southeast of Poros just where you "turn the corner" into Kolpos Idhras. They are not easily identified from the distance if you are hugging the coast from Poros harbour and you will not see the gap between Skilli and Spathi until up to Ak Spathi. The gap between the two islands is much used as a short-cut by yachts and by hydrofoils and ferries. The channel is deep and clear of dangers in the fairway but considerable caution is needed to keep clear of the hydrofoils and ferries using it especially as they seem to appear out of nowhere. Care must also be taken not to confuse the navigable channel with that between Nisis Spathi and the coast which is obstructed by a reef - from the south this gap and not the navigable channel will often be the first you see.

On the south side of Nisis Spathi there is an isolated anchorage affording better shelter from the prevailing wind than appears on the chart.

Nisidhes Tselevinia. The gap between the two islands is much used as a short-cut and care is needed of hydrofoils and ferries charging through at speed.

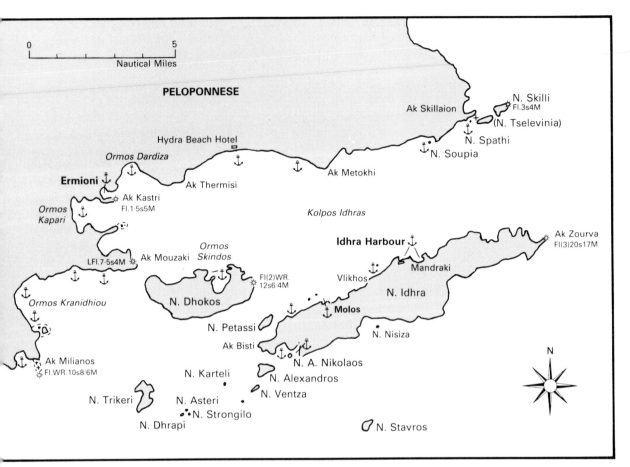

Anchor tucked in next to the islet where convenient. Open to the south. There is a tiny monastery or church immediately west which appears to be occupied.

Ak Skillaion, the cape reaching out to Nisis Spathi, is presumed to be the cape where Minos, the first king of Crete (hence the Minoans) threw the besotted Scylla overboard. Minos defeated the Megarans and Athenians in battle because of the treachery of the Megaran kings' daughter Scylla. After betraying her father for love of Minos she embarked with him bound for Crete. For whatever reason Minos ordered his Cretan crew to throw her overboard and it is here that she was washed up- a not unreasonable place as a great deal of flotsam and jetsam collects at this corner.

The story ends on a macabre note as Pausanias relates: "They show you no grave; her neglected body was torn to pieces they say by the sea birds".

Pausanias goes on to give the following description of sailing from Skillaion to Ermioni.

"Sailing from Skillaion towards the city you come to the Ox's head, another cape, and then to the islands beyond it, first Salt Island which offers an anchorage, then Pine Island, and thirdly Left Hand Island. As you sail past them another cape called the obstacle sticks out from the mainland, then comes Three-Headed Island, and a mountain projecting into the sea from the Peloponnese, called the Ox-Crossing, with a sanctuary on it to Demeter and her

Tselevinia on the corner where you turn into Kolpos Idhras.

daughter and to Athene Guardian of the Anchorage. Offshore lies an island called Deceit, with another called Water Island not far away. From here the beaches of the mainland curve away in a crescent ending in Poseidonion (at Ermioni).
Pausanias Guide to Greece Vol 1 transl. Peter Levi.

Numerous explanations have been put forward to explain these references. One (Leake) claims the ship Pausanias was in sailed right around Idhra and arrived at Ermioni from the south. Another claims Pausanias was misreading the sailing directions of the time. None of these complicated solutions are necessary as any sailor in a small boat navigating his way along the coast will quickly

appreciate. The prominent objects from seawards are not always apparent from looking at a chart although retrospectively they can be identified.

Thus the Ox's Head is the small prominent headland (now with a church on it) less than a mile after Spathi. Salt Island is Soupia which does indeed have an anchorage behind it. Pine Island is probably Ak Metokhi which has silted and is now connected to the coast - there are lagoons around it and pine and other trees grow nearby sustained by a spring. Left-hand Island is Idhra. The Obstacle is Ak Thermisi which it would be as you headed into the large bay and perhaps had to tack out in southeast winds. Three-Headed Island is Dhokos with three conspicuous capes. The Ox-Crossing could be Ak Mouzaki and the islands of Deceit and Water Island could be any of Trikeri, Spetsai, or Spetsopoula. The crescent beaches could be either Dardiza or Kapari.

Of course this is all as speculative as the guesses anyone else might make, but at this time we know there were primitive charts and I pin my faith on skippers of the time who would be very careful not to increase distance and danger by sailing around Idhra to Ermioni - I'm fairly confident the route was a well known one and the skipper plugged along the coast by the shortest route to Ermioni.

Nisis Soupia

An islet usually called Frog Island, it does indeed look like a crouching frog, though the name *soupia* actually means cuttlefish which it does not in the least resemble. Behind the islet there is an anchorage well sheltered from the prevailing wind. The bottom is covered in thick weed and is poor holding in parts.

In the eastern entrance there is a miniature cove with room for about one yacht with a long line ashore or anchored fore and aft in idyllic surroundings.

Frog island - it does look a bit like a crouching frog - on the northern side of Kolpos Idhras.

Ak Methoki

A low sandy cape. In calm weather or light easterlies a yacht can anchor on the west side of the cape off the long sandy beach. The bottom shelves gently in. The water-boat for Idhra has a jetty on the east side of the cape.

Idhra Beach Hotel

A hotel development near Plepi about 7 miles west of Nisis Soupia. It takes it's name from Idhra, no doubt to cash in on the charm and fame of the island across the water, though it bears little resemblance to the architecture on Idhra.

There is a small harbour off the hotel complex (2 metre depths just inside) but it is normally crowded with tripper boats. In calm weather or light easterlies it is possible to anchor off the hotel complex. Restaurants and bars ashore.

Ormos Dardiza

The large bay immediately northeast of Ermioni. In calm weather or light easterlies a yacht can anchor off the beach. It is quite deep until close in and you will usually have to anchor in around 10 metres on mud and weed, patchy holding in places. Although it looks like

shelter should be good from even strong easterlies in fact a swell is pushed around the corner into the bay. In the northeast corner there is a disused loading gantry and a taverna opens in the summer.

Ermioni (Hermione)

The village in the far northwest corner of Kolpos Idhras with a skinny headland sheltering the bay and harbour.

Pilotage

Approach The buildings of the village straddling the headland are conspicuous from both the east and the south. Closer in the headland and the light structure on it are easily identified and once into the bay the harbour will be seen. Care needs to be taken of the submerged ancient mole on the south side of the bay. Numerous ferries and hydrofoils stop at Ermioni and a lookout should be kept for them.

Mooring Go stern or bows-to behind the outer short pier. The bottom is mud and weed, good holding. Good shelter from all winds behind here. If it is crowded behind the pier it is possible to go bows-to the outer end of north quay under the breakwater. Care is needed as depths are irregular and rock ballasting extends underwater from the quay in places. It

Approach to Ermioni looking west.

can be very uncomfortable here with easterlies which send in a swell side-on causing boats to roll badly and it can be better to anchor off north of the breakwater.

Facilities

Services Water on the quay. Fuel delivered by mini-tanker.

Provisions Good shopping for all provisions nearby. Ice available.

Eating Out Good tavernas on the waterfront and on the south side of the headland.

Other PO. Metered telephone. Hire motorbikes. Ferries and hydrofoils to Piraeus and south.

General

The village is a quiet place after the bustle of the islands and well worth the slight detour off the nautical motor way linking the main islands. It has some tourism but not too much yet though a number of the ubiquitous blank square concrete hotels of what have been described as the pour-and-fill variety have been erected. The headland on which the ancient city stood is now a pine-clad park which at sunset, with the scent of pine needles in the air, is the perfect place for a pre-prandial stroll. Over the saddle of the hill on the south side of the village the local fishing boats are moored and an old fashioned *cafeneion* by the quay is the perfect place for a beer or an *ouzo* before dinner.

Tip of the skinny headland sheltering the anchorage and harbour on the north side of Ermioni.

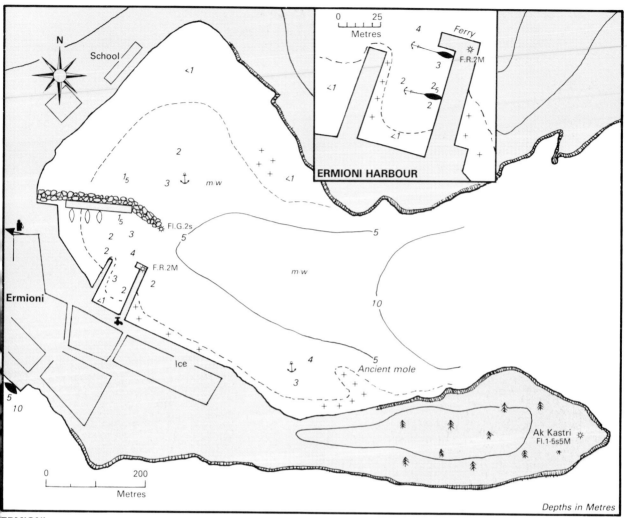

ERMIONI HARBOUR

Depths in Metres

ERMIONI
37°23'·2N 23°15'E (F.R.2M)

Ancient Ermioni (or Hermione) was evidently a place of some consequence if the number of temples and the space allotted it in Pausanias' guide are anything to go by. It possessed three important temples and the city itself was ringed by a high wall. Little remains today of the city although chunks of ancient masonry can be identified on the headland and built into some of the older buildings. The temples had some strange rites recorded by Pausanias.

Ermioni. The anchorage in the north bay.

Ermioni. The small harbour on the north side.

At a small shrine to Aphrodite all virgins and widows intending to go with a man had to perform a sacrifice - a sort of early version of church bans. On the headland was a colonnade called Echo's Colonnade where any word was repeated three times. In a temple to Demeter four old women resided, guardians of a shrine and statue inside which no-one else, foreigner or resident of the city, was allowed to see. At the festival to Demeter four perfect heifers were driven into the temple and slaughtered with a sickle by the old women. Now we know where Hollywood got its material for its horror movies.

Off the north side of the headland in a small bight are the remains of the ancient harbour.

The city had numerous maritime links. The principal temple to Aphrodite on the headland was dedicated to "Aphrodite of the Deep Sea and the Harbour". Pausanias mentions that there were several harbours on the north side and it may be that the present harbour includes an ancient mole.

There is an interesting reference in Pausanias to a festival held here that is unique. It was held every year in honour of Dionysus and included "a musical contest in his honour, and prizes for a diving competition and a boat-race". This is the earliest reference to a boat race that we have and if true Ermioni was probably the site of the first recorded regatta in history. However there are problems over the

Retsina barrels ready for soaking in
the sea on the south quay at Ermioni.

translation of the word for "boat-race" and it
may mean a swimming race. Still it is a pleasant
caprice on a sultry summer evening to sit on the
headland and muse on what the boats might
have looked like racing around the bay.

Ermioni South Quay

In calm weather it is possible to go stern or
bows-to the south fisherman's quay, after first
enquiring if you are not taking a local boats
place. With southerlies or easterlies the quay
becomes untenable and you should move
around to the north side of the headland.

Ormos Kapari

In calm weather or light southerlies a yacht can
anchor off the beach in Ormos Kapari. Anchor
in 3-8 metres where convenient with the
southwest corner normally giving the best
shelter. The bottom is mud and weed, good
holding.

Off the southern entrance point of the bay
care is needed of Nisidhes Kapari, an islet with
some isolated rocks just above water to the east
of it. In calm weather there is a pleasant
anchorage under the islet taking care of the reef
to the west of it.

Ormos Kouverta

An indifferent anchorage south of Ormos
Kouverta. In calm weather anchor off the north
side.

Nisis Idhra

This stark mountainous island lying along the southern edge of Kolpos Idhras gives no indication of human habitation or even the possibility of it until closer to you see a few white houses dotted here and there. It oozes prehistory although no prehistoric remains have been found and in fact it was not until comparatively recent times, in the 18th century, that it worked it's way into the history books. The ancient world effectively passed it by.

The barren precipitous slopes become friendlier on closer association. Houses and monasteries can be identified. At the southern end the lower slopes are clothed in pine. But the port and town of Idhra, the only significant settlement, are hidden in a defile and cannot be seen until you are nearly up to the entrance. The closed book opens and the port and town are revealed suddenly and dramatically - especially to the navigator approaching it for the first time who may have been wondering just where the harbour was.

The island has probably been a refuge for pirates and those on the periphery of society for a long time. Herodotus relates that Ermioni sold the island to refugees from Samos in the 6th century BC but they soon despaired of doing anything with it and moved on to Crete. The name of the island, probably derived from Hydrea, "a watering place", is paradoxical as there are no significant springs on the island. In the 16th and 17th centuries refugees fleeing from the mainland settled at Kiapha on the hill above the harbour. These were probably of Albanian origin as Kiapha is Albanian for "a

Caique coaster docking at Idhra.

head" or "summit". The settlement flourished in its own modest way and soon the inhabitants began to indulge in modest trading voyages to the Peloponnese. The small vessels for this were mostly built locally and as the profits from the trading voyages increased larger vessels, up to fifty and sixty tons, were built. The smaller vessels would have been lateen rigged but larger vessels were schooners or small brigantines.

The island was little affected by the Ottoman conquest of the Peloponnese. It was of little significance or threat - or so it appeared. When an Ottoman fleet anchored off Ak Metokhi to take on water the Grand Vizier, Damad Ali, was surprised to receive a delegation from the apparently deserted island. The Idhriots pledged not to interfere in Ottoman matters and the Ottomans in turn were content to leave the Idhriots alone and to collect an annual tax. Idhriots served in the Ottoman fleet and Ottoman ships were repaired in the island shipyard. The ship owners prospered and under Russian protection ran profitable cargoes of grain from the Black Sea to the Aegean. A little privateering on the side brought in nearly as much revenue and British captains cursed the piratical Idhriots and suggested in dispatches that Idhriot ships should be blown out of the water despite Russian protection. Most of the mansions around the port were built in this prosperous era at the beginning of the 19th century.

Although Byron is often thought of as an out-and-out Philhellene, he had a canny understanding of the Greeks that these verses from *Don Juan*, though placed in an anonymous Aegean island, I think apply perfectly to Idhra and the Idhriots of the time.

A fisherman he had been in his youth,
And still a sort of fisherman was he.
But other speculations were, in sooth,
Added to his connection with the sea,
Perhaps not so respectable, in truth.
A little smuggling and some piracy
Left him at last the sole of many masters
Of an ill-gotten million of piastres.

19th century engraving of Idhra (Linton).

A fisher therefore was he, though of men,
Like Peter the Apostle, and he fished
For wandering merchant vessels now and then
And sometimes caught as many as he wished.
The cargoes he confiscated, and gain
He sought in the slave market too and dished
Full many a morsel for that Turkish trade,
By which no doubt a good deal he made.
Don Juan Lord Byron

The Idhriots were reluctant to join the Greek War of Independence - after all they enjoyed good relations with the Ottomans and had prospered handsomely from it. In 1821 things came to a head when a group of unemployed sailors and captains caused the town council to resign and make over the Idhriot fleet to the Greek cause. The small ships carrying few cannon could not hope to take on the Turks wholesale and developed the art of the fire ship to perfection. An old ship was covered in tar, littered with kindling and barrels of gunpowder, and then sailed by a skeleton crew into the Turkish fleet where it was set on fire. The crew escaped on a small cutter towed behind. The Turks never found an answer to the fire ship and the small Idhriot fleet along with the Spetsiots caused disproportionate damage for all their few ships.

The end of the war spelled disaster for Idhra. The fleet was decimated. The new Greek government clamped down on privateering.

Idhra town quay.

There were no blockades to run for big profits. New boats could not be financed and new technology in the shape of the steam engine was undermining old sailing skills. Idhra declined and in 1842 there was only a population of 4000 left compared with 28,000 in the 1820's. The town and port were left a shell that until the trickle of tourism in the 1960's remained much as it had been in the early 19th century.

Limin Idhra

The harbour and town are tucked into a cove approximately in the middle of the north coast of the island.

Pilotage

Approach Though the harbour and the main part of the town cannot be seen until you are right up to it, the houses straddling the ridge on either side and up the slopes behind the town can be distinguished. The numerous ferries and hydrofoils entering and leaving the harbour will also be seen. Closer in the town and harbour mole will be seen. Care needs to be taken of the ferries and hydrofoils entering and leaving as well as tripper boats, water taxis and other boats. The entrance is quite narrow and care is needed of traffic jams in the immediate approach.

Mooring Idhra is a popular destination and if you want to be assured of a berth in the summer, especially at weekends, you will need to be here by two or three in the afternoon. Go stern or bows-to the mole or the south quay. It is best to be on the north quay as although shelter is normally good, with strong northerlies the harbour is like a washing machine and the only place to be is on the north quay along the mole. At the height of summer boats are commonly banked three out from the quay and crossed anchors and cross tempers are commonplace. The bottom is mud and weed, good holding although as just mentioned you will probably be over someone's anchor or they will be over yours.

Idhra harbour looking from the eastern side. Nigel Patten

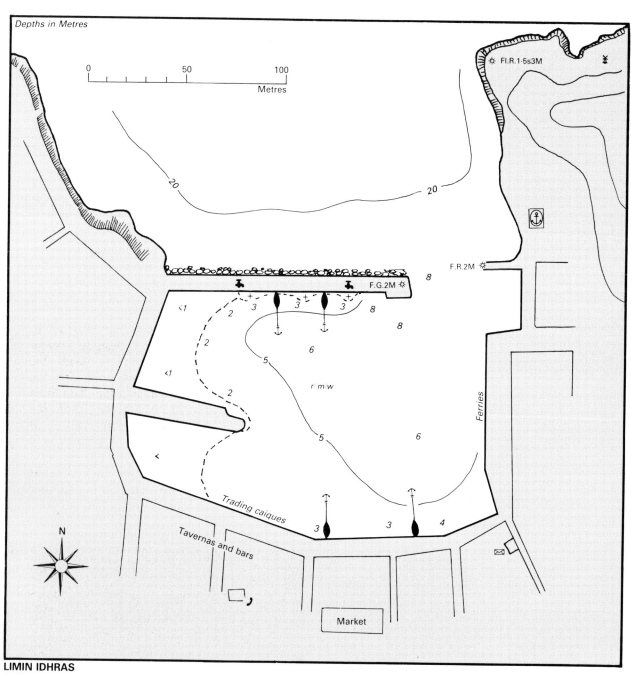

Depths in Metres

0   50   100

Metres

FI.R.1·5s3M

20   20

F.R.2M

8

F.G.2M

<1   2   3   3   3   8

2   8

2   6

<1   5

2   r/m/w

5   6

5   6

Ferries

<

3   3   4

Trading caiques

Tavernas and bars

Market

N

LIMIN IDHRAS
37°21′·1N 23°28′E (F.G.2M)

The entrance to Idhra harbour - difficult to spot for the first time until the closed book opens and the town and harbour are revealed.

Facilities

Services Water on the quay.

Provisions Good shopping for provisions. There is a small market just behind the south quay. Ice available.

Eating Out Numerous tavernas of all types. In from the southeast corner of the harbour *The Well* is recommended for its country-style dishes. Close by is a simple taverna. The *El Greco* is also recommended. I suggest you stay away from anywhere, especially the bars, on the waterfront where excessive prices and faked bonhomie are the rule. There are some good bars further into town.

Other PO. OTE. Water taxis. Ferries and hydrofoils to Piraeus and west and south.

General

The trouble with Idhra is that you and everyone else wants to see it and in the height of summer it is over-crowded. By day cruise ships and ferries pour people into the place. By night fenders pop and the amphitheatre of a harbour is choked with the fumes from the generators of motorboats. There must be more souvenir-gift-gold-jewellery shops per square metre in Idhra than anywhere else. And you already know what I think of the bars on the waterfront where it is assumed any spare change is a tip.

And yet you must see it. It is a museum town that has changed little since its abrupt change of fortune in the mid-19th century. The mansions packed around the harbour are elegant examples of 19th century ship-owners houses built before the age of the motor vehicle and because there are so few places to go there are still virtually no motor vehicles on the island except for the refuse truck and a couple of cars which were rumoured to have had a head-on collision recently.

The majority of the mansions, known as *archontiki*, were to Italian designs though executed by Greek stonemasons, with the western slopes the favoured spot for the wealthy. One of the largest, the Tombazis house, is now part of the Athens School of Fine Arts. Any building work now is carried on in much the same way as the past (thanks to a historical preservation order) with the raw materials brought in by *caique* and unloaded onto the pier on the west side of the harbour

Idhra. Mansions on the east side of the harbour.

from where it is transported by donkey-power around the town and outskirts. If you want to get anywhere inland and feel disinclined to walk then donkeys are the only alternative.

In the 1960's the town attracted the disaffected and disillusioned and a few artists as well. One who combined disillusion with art was Leonard Cohen who lived on the island for a while and composed his suicidal ballads here - he still has a house here by all accounts. Gradually the attractions of the place grew until the present and the numbers now visiting here daily must run into thousands. Out of season, in spring and autumn, there are fewer visitors and the place is more amenable- and you have a better chance of arriving late and finding a berth.

Idhra. Inner *caique* basin.

Mandraki

A bay approximately ¾ of a mile east of Idhra harbour. It offers reasonable shelter from the prevailing winds. Anchor in 8-15 metres keeping clear of the area buoyed off for swimmers. The bottom is mud and weed, reasonable holding. Easterlies blowing down the gulf send some swell in here, more uncomfortable than dangerous, and the bay is open north.

Ashore there is a small hotel and restaurant. Mandraki has one of the few sandy patches that can be called a beach on Idhra and tripper boats run around to here from the town. Mandraki means a "sheepfold" or a "small enclosure" and in the 19th century this was an alternative port

Mandraki on Idhra.

when the town harbour was full. It also had several boatyards building and repairing the sailing ships and a small boatyard for local *caiques* remains today.

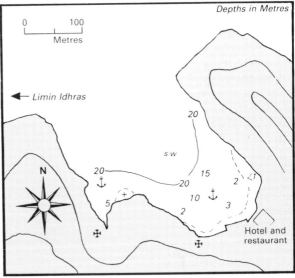

MANDRAKI
37°21'N 23°29'E

Anchorages around Nisos Idhra

Depending on the wind and sea there are a number of anchorages around Idhra that can be used.

Ormos Molos. A small cove approximately 3 miles southwest of Limin Idhras. Anchor and take a long line ashore - normally to the west side. There is reasonable shelter from the prevailing winds in here with the two outlying islets providing some additional shelter. Open to the north when a swell is pushed in.

Petassi anchorage. In calm weather there is a cove suitable for a lunch stop approximately half a mile east of the east end of Nisis Petassi.

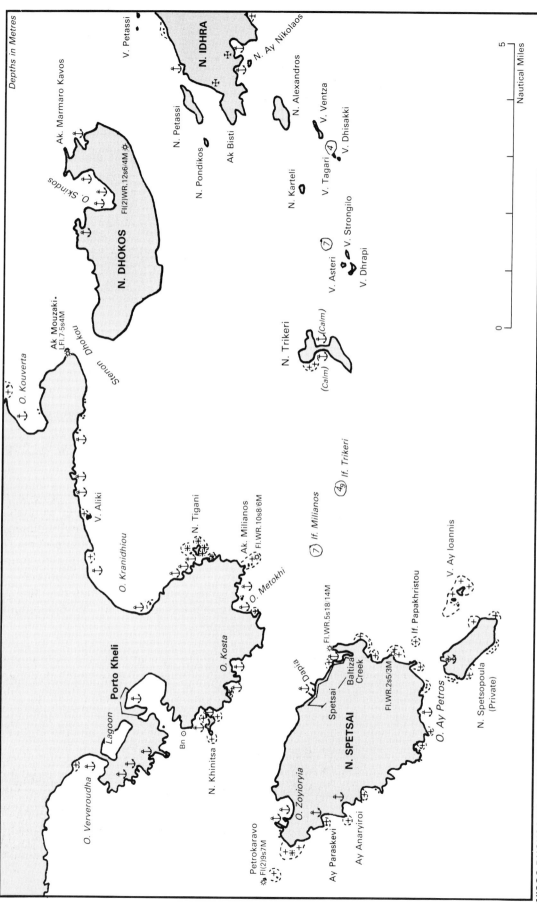

NISOS DHOKOS TO NISOS SPETSAI

Depths in Metres

Nautical Miles

0   5

N. IDHRA

V. Petassi

Ak. Marmaro Kavos

N. Ay Nikolaos

O. Skindos

N. Petassi

Ak Bisti

N. Pondikos

N. Alexandros

V. Ventza

N. DHOKOS

Fl(2)WR.12s6/4M

V. Tagari ④

V. Dhisakki

N. Karteli

V. Asteri ⑦

V. Strongilo

Ak. Mouzaki.
LFl.7·5s4M

Stenon Dhokou

N. Trikeri

↓(Calm)

V. Dhrapi

O. Kouverta

(Calm) ↓

O. Kranidhiou

V. Aliki

If. Trikeri ④₉

N. Tigani

If. Milianos ④₉

Ak. Milianos
Fl.WR.10s8·6M

O. Metokhi

If. Milianos ⑦

O. Kosta

Porto Kheli

Lagoon

Bn ○

Fl.WR.5s18/14M

V. Ay Ioannis

Dapia

N. Khinitsa

Spetsai

Baltiza
Creek

If. Papakhristou

O. Ververoudha

O. Zoyioryia

N. SPETSAI

Fl.WR.2s5/3M

O. Ay Petros

N. Spetsopoula
(Private)

Petrokaravo
☀ Fl(2)9s7M

Ay Paraskevi

Ay Anaryiroi

The chapel on Kamini rock just southwest of Idhra harbour.

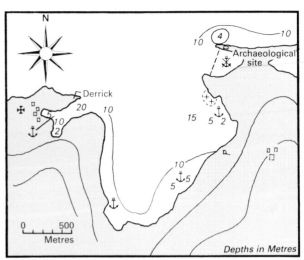

ORMOS SKINDOS
37°20'·5N 23°20'E

Ormos Ay Nikolaos. On the southwest end of Idhra there is a large bay bisected by a headland and an islet Nisis Ay Nikolaos. A smallchapel by the shore will be seen. Anchor in either bay. With the southeast wind in the afternoon a swell rolls into the two bays.

Nisis Dhokos

The high barren island lying between the southwest end of Idhra and the coast of the Peloponnese. If Idhra appears bare and barren and uninhabited then Dhokos appears even more so. On the south side the slopes drop precipitously to the sea leaving only a small rocky spur on the southeast for the little light-house to sit on. On the north side the slopes are less steep, but only marginally so. The island belongs to a number of Idhriot families and was formerly used for quarrying marble. A derrick still sits on the west side of the entrance to the Ormos Skindos. There are a number of anchorages around Ormos Skindos, the large bay on the north.

Dhokos Cove. The small inlet just inside the western entrance of Ormos Skindos. It is quite deep for anchoring and you will have to drop your anchor in 6-15 metres and take a long line ashore to the north side of the inlet. Care is needed as the large mooring chain to which a buoy was formerly attached still lies on the

bottom and if you foul it there is no chance of lifting it to free the anchor. Ashore is a hamlet though only a few houses are occupied in the summer.

Ormos Skindos. In settled weather boats anchor anywhere around the large bay with a long line ashore. Care is needed in the northeast corner where a reef fringes the coast.

Archaeological site In the very northeast of Ormos Skindos is a cove sheltered by a thin finger of land. This area is an archaeological site and normally buoyed off in the summer. It is out of bounds and so it should be. The site is believed to be a Hellenic harbour, possibly of the 5th or 6th century BC, though it is strange no mention is made of it by ancient commentators.

Derrick on the west side of the entrance to Ormos Skindos.

Dhokos cove.

East Cove. In calm weather there is a cove on the east side of the island that can be used. When easterlies blow down the gulf it becomes untenable.

Note In the sea area between Idhra and Dhokos there is often a period of variable light winds or calm when on either side there is a good breeze blowing. It is best to motor through this patch and pick up the breeze on the other side.

Nisis Trikeri

The island lying almost midway between Idhra and Spetsai. Fishing boats will often be seen around it and in calm weather a yacht can anchor on either side of the isthmus joining the two halves.

Between Trikeri and Idhra are several other islets and rocks. Proceeding west from Idhra these are Nisis Alexandros, Nisis Ventza, Vrakhonisos Tagari and Dhisakki, Nisis Karteli, and Vrakhonisos Strongilo, Asteri, and Dhrapi just east of Trikeri itself.

Ak Mouzaki on the north side of the channel between Dhokos and the Peloponnese.

The coast from Ak Mouzaki to Porto Kheli

Ormos Kranidhiou

Around Ak Mouzaki is the large bay of Kranidhiou. In calm weather and light southerlies or northerlies there are several places a yacht can anchor around the bay.

North Side. In calm weather anchor where convenient off the north side of the bay. The bottom shelves up nearly everywhere to convenient depths but there are several small coves east of Vrakhonisos Aliki which are usually favoured.

Northwest Head. At the head of the bay the bottom shelves gently to the low-lying shore. In calm weather anchor off where convenient. In the southwest corner some shelter can be gained from light southeasterlies.

West Side. Anchor off in any of the coves on the west side where there is some shelter from light southeasterlies. There is also an anchorage behind Nisis Tigani. Numbers of villas have been built along the coast.

Anchorage on the north side of Ormos Kranidhiou.

Ak Milianos.

Ak Milianos

The cape with a chapel on it is easily identified. Now there is a light structure on the end of the reef (Vrakhoi Kounoupia) running out from the cape fewer boats are tempted to cut the corner and come to a grinding halt - as long as you pass to seawards of the light structure.

Ifalos Milianos and Trikeri

Two reefs lying approximately 1.½ miles (If. Milianos) south of the cape and 2 miles (If. Trikeri) southeast of the cape. Ifalos Milianos has 7 metres least depth over it and Ifalos Trikeri 4.9 metres least depth so they are really only of concern to deep draught vessels.

Ormos Methoki

The bay immediately west of Ak Milianos. Care is needed on the east side of the bay which is bordered by shoal water and a small islet. Yachts can anchor around the bay where convenient as the bottom shelves up to the shore though care is needed in one or two places where reefs border the coast. The prevailing wind will not always blow home into here and some yachts stay overnight.

Ormos Kosta

The next bay approximately a mile west of Metokhi and the mainland terminal for the ferry to Spetsai. The prevailing wind normally pushes a swell into here but in calm weather or light southeasterlies a yacht can anchor off where convenient.

Immediately west of Kosta is another bay which can be used in calm weather. Care is needed of the reef off the west entrance point.

Nisis Khinitsa

A low barren islet lying close to the east entrance point of Porto Kheli. Behind the islet a yacht can anchor in 4-5 metre depths on sand. Here there is good protection from the prevailing southeasterly blowing up the Spetsai Channel and consequently it is popular in the summer. You can also tuck into the coves on the mainland coast behind the islet though care is needed of the depths in places.

STENON SPETSAI

N

0   2
Nautical Miles

Porto Kheli

The large circular landlocked bay opposite Spetsai.

Pilotage

Approach It is difficult to determine exactly where the entrance is for the first time although in the summer the numbers of boats coming and going and the hydrofoils and water taxis entering and leaving give a fairly good clue. Closer in the light structure on the west side and the stone beacon marking the reef on the east side will be seen. Once into the entrance everything falls into place and entry into the bay proper is straightforward. Care is needed of the hydrofoils and water taxis and other boats using the bay and although it is perfectly feasible to sail in, keep an eagle eye out for other craft.

Mooring Go stern or bows-to the northern half of the quay or anchor off. In the north part of

the bay are numerous laid moorings for craft kept here and several buoyed areas for swimmers and water-skiers, so care is needed when choosing a spot to anchor. Alternatively anchor in the southeast corner. The bottom is gooey mud and excellent holding though make sure your anchor is well in if going on the quay as the prevailing wind blows straight onto it. The bay is a "hurricane hole" as far as shelter goes and shelter from all winds is good apart from the fetch across the bay which can make it bumpy on the quay in strong southeasterlies and uncomfortable in the southeast corner with strong northerlies.

Facilities

Services Water delivered by tanker and fuel by mini-tanker. The water on the quay is brackish.

The rough stone beacon on the southeast side of the channel leading into Porto Kheli.

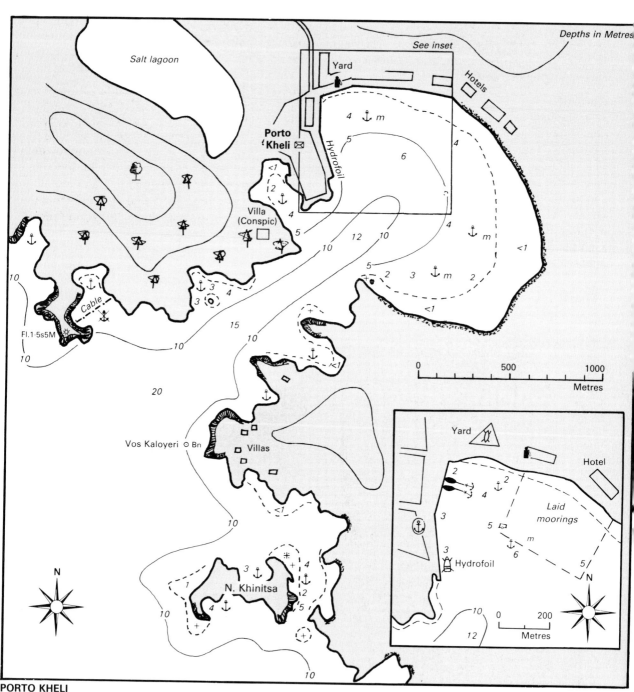

Depths in Metres

Salt lagoon

See inset

Yard

Hotels

Porto
Kheli

Hydrofoil

4 m

5

6

4

Villa
(Conspic)

<1

2

4

5

4 m

<1

10

12 10

5

2 3 m 2

<1

15

10

Cable

Fl.1·5s5M

10

10

10

20

Vos Kaloyeri ⊙ Bn

Villas

<1

10

N. Khinitsa

3

+ 4

1

+ 2

4

5

10

+

10

Inset:

Yard

Hotel

2

4

2

Laid
moorings

3

5

3

6

5

3 Hydrofoil

N

10

0   200

12

Metres

0   500   1000

Metres

N

Provisions Good shopping for all provisions in the village. Ice available.

Eating Out Numerous tavernas in the town and around the northern shore.

Other PO. OTE. Hire motorbikes and cars. Hydrofoils and catamaran ferry to Piraeus and points along the way and to the south.

General

Kheli means eel and presumably there were once lots of them here though I suspect it is a reference to the lagoon immediately west of the port which is a fish farm and was probably once connected on the east to the harbour. In the southeast are a few ruins and a necropolis of ancient Alice (Halice or Aleis) of which next to nothing is known and about which next to nothing is said by ancient commentators, so apparently it was of little importance though you would have thought the natural harbour would have warranted a sizeable settlement. The quayed area and bulldozed strip behind it were initially built in the 1960's for a NATO base which was subsequently scrapped.

Porto Kheli is tailor made for watersports so it is no surprise a number of hotels have been built around its shores and that the bay itself is a riot of fluorescent wind surfer sails, dinghy sails, water-ski boats and parascending boats. Swimmers take refuge in buoyed off areas and pedalos occasionally venture into the watersport maelstrom outside the buoys. Yachtsmen should take care not to run-over dilettante wind surfers and wobbly skiers and in turn should take care not to get run down by gin palaces and hydrofoils.

Porto Kheli

Porto Kheli looking from the slopes on the north side of the bay.

Anchorages around Porto Kheli

East Side of the Entrance. There are two coves here in which yachts can anchor although several craft on permanent moorings take up the best places.

West Side of the Entrance. A bay with an above water rock in it is often used although at the time of writing a recent wreck just behind the rock was putting people off. It was buoyed by what looked like a fish-box. It is still possible to get into the head and take a long line ashore.

Light Structure Cove. The cove immediately east of the light structure at the entrance. Although in an area where anchoring is prohibited because of underwater cables it has been used as long for a long time and no-one seems to object. Anchor near the head of the bay.

Kiln Bay. The cove immediately west of the light structure. Reasonable shelter from the prevailing winds.

Headland Bay. The cove just northwest of Kiln Bay. The headland looks like an islet from some directions. Anchor in 2-5 metres on sand and weed. Good shelter from the prevailing winds in here.

Just northwest is another cove which also affords reasonable shelter from the prevailing winds.

West side bay in Porto Kheli.

Nisos Spetsai

This relatively low-lying island lies just south of Porto Kheli separated by a channel just over a mile across. Spetsai is nowhere very high reaching just 276 metres (899 ft) at its summit and the pine forest covering most of the island softens its outline still more. It was known as Pityoussa, the "pine tree island", to Pausanias, a name thought (though I don't see the connection) to give rise to the present one of Spetses or Spetsai. However the covering of pine it now has is not ancient but the product of a reforestation programme implemented at the turn of the century.

In common with much of the surrounding area, Spetsai has no ancient associations that we know of. Like Idhra it was not until the 18th century that migrants from the Peloponnese settled here and like Idhra the island was little known even to Greeks until the war effort

earlier than Idhra, indeed it was the Spetsiot example which spurred Idhra to Greek War of Independence. Spetsai joined the adopt the cause, and committed her fleet to fighting the Ottoman navy scoring some notable successes under the direction of the island's heroine Boubalina.

Born Lascarina Boubalina in Idhra to a sea captain, she grew up with a passionate interest in the sea and ships. Not surprisingly she married a sea captain from Spetsai and accompanied him on his voyages. She got through two more husbands before the War of Independence and managed to have nine children and accumulate a large fleet of ships courtesy of the three husbands. Her most daring exploit was to force the surrender of the Turkish garrison at Navplion with hardly a shot being fired. She simply sailed up to Navplion and threatened to send fire-ships into the Turkish fleet. The Turks surrendered straight away.

Spetsiot caique.
From a painting on wood.

Caique yard at Baltiza. Yards here are said to build the best *caiques* in Greece.

She was feted all over Greece and so many legends grew up about her exploits, especially her sexual appetite, that it is hard to separate fact from fiction.

With the war won Spetsai declined and languished until the return of a native son at the turn of the century. Sotiros Anagyros was born on Spetsai but left to make his fortune which he did returning a millionaire. Inspired no doubt by Pausanias' description of a pine-clad island (though we cannot be certain his description is of Spetsai) he embarked on a massive project to replant most of the island with Aleppo pine. He also built the first hotel on the island, the *Poseidonion*, and the exclusive boys boarding school staffed by teachers from the British Council. Anagyros was generally not liked by the natives for his high-handed changes to the island though his heart was in the right place.

On his death the estate (most of the island) passed to a trust.

Sadly fire recently destroyed much of the pine forest on the western side of the island and the boys school was closed down in 1984 though there is talk of turning it into a conference centre.

In the 1950's one of the teachers delegated to the school was the young John Fowles and aficionados of his writing will know that Spetsai is the setting for *The Magus*. The *House of the Magus* or *Bourani* where much of the action takes place is the large *Villa Yasemia* on the west coast above Ay Paraskevi. John Fowles has said that *The Magus* embodied more of what he was trying to get across than his later novels and he later revised the ending to it in line with how he thought it should end rather than how the publishers thought it should.

Today the island has a fair amount of tourism though it is not overburdened by it. Despite the recent fire much of the island is still covered by pine and there are pleasant walks or you can cycle around the island. The enlightened policies of Anagyros banned motor vehicles from Spetsai and though in recent years a few have crept in, most transport is still by horse-drawn gharry. There is something ineluctably old-fashioned and wonderful about clip-clopping back from a good meal to the harbour.

Getting around inland

Basically there is a single ring road around the island with a few interconnecting tracks in the interior. If you want to do a circuit there are either bicycles or motorbikes for hire - the fit should take bicycles and boycott the motorbikes which have only recently been allowed on the island so ensure that Anagyros doesn't get too restless in his grave. For getting back and forth from Baltiza and the Dapia gharries can be used. There is an intermittent bus service running along the north side of the island and a couple of taxis.

Horse-drawn gharry on Spetsai.

Baltiza

The inlet on the northeast end of the island where a yacht should make for rather than the ferry port off the town proper.

Pilotage

Approach The houses of Spetsai spreading from the Dapia around and over Ak Fanari are easily identified. Closer in the lighthouse on Ak Fanari and several windmills (now converted to houses) are easily identified. Care is needed of the short reef and shoal water off the end of Ak Fanari. With the prevailing southeasterlies there is often a confused rolling swell at the entrance though it is flat inside the outer harbour.

Mooring Anchor in the outer harbour with a long line ashore to the east or the west side.

The bottom is mud, sand and weed, reasonable holding. The inner harbour is normally crowded in the summer but you may find a berth double or triple-banked out. Crossed anchors are virtually unavoidable in the inner harbour. Shelter in the outer harbour is reasonable although strong southeasterlies cause a surge. Shelter in the inner harbour is excellent although the water-taxis cause a lot of wash zooming in and out.

Facilities

Services Water and fuel on the quay tucked just inside in the inner harbour.

Provisions Good shopping for provisions nearby.

Eating Out Numerous tavernas nearby and in the town. A speciality of the island is *Psari Spetsiotiko*, "Fish of Spetsai", which is a fish

Baltiza creek.

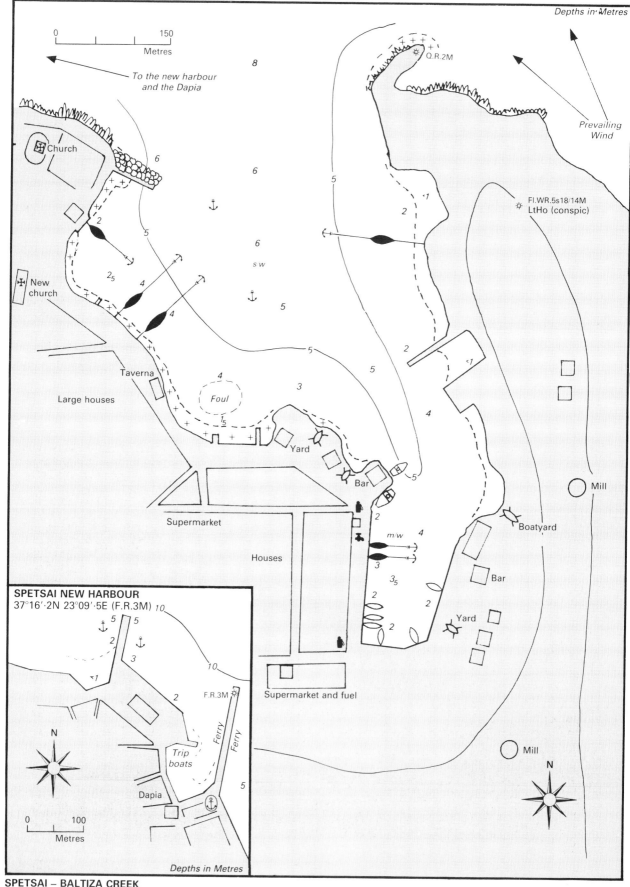

0   150
Metres

To the new harbour
and the Dapia

8

Q.R.2M

Prevailing
Wind

⊞ Church

6

6

6

6

s w

5

Fl.WR.5s18/14M
LtHo (conspic)

✠ New
church

2

2₅   4

4

4

5

5

5

2

5

Taverna

Large houses

4
Foul

3

1
5

Yard

Bar

2

m/w

3

4

4

Boatyard

Supermarket

Houses

3

3₅

Bar

2

Mill

2

2

Yard

SPETSAI NEW HARBOUR
37°16'·2N 23°09'·5E (F.R.3M)   10

5   5

2

3

10

1

2   F.R.3M

Ferry   Ferry

Trip
boats

Supermarket and fuel

N

Dapia

5

0   100
Metres

Mill

N

Depths in Metres

SPETSAI – BALTIZA CREEK
37°16N 23°10'E (Q.R.2M)

such as bream cooked in a casserole with tomatoes, stock, and cheese. *Haralambos* on the road around the outer harbour has good fish as does *Trehandiri* nearby. It is well worth the effort to grab a gharry and go to *Klimataria* inland at Analipsis - a wide variety of *mezes* are served and the best idea is just to ask for a selection and let everyone dip in until sated.

Other PO. OTE. Banks. Hire motorbikes and bicycles. Ferries and hydrofoils to Piraeus and south.

General

Baltiza is something of an oasis away from the bustle of the Dapia although at night some of the bars turn the volume up a bit too much. The various small yards around the harbour haul and built *caiques* reputed to be amongst the best in Greece.

Tim Severin had his replica of an early Greek scouting ship built here for his voyages following the track of Jason and the Argonauts and the wanderings of Odysseus. It was built using traditional methods, building the outside planking first and inserting the ribs later, using wooden pegs to join the planks edge to edge, soaking the wood in the sea to bend it into shape, until finally a replica of a Homeric scouting galley was launched into Spetsai harbour.

Above the harbour and lining the road into town are numerous *archontiki*, the rich merchants houses like those on Idhra built during Spetsai's economic boom in the early 19th century. Above the outer harbour is the Monastery of Aghios Nikolaos, established as a monastery in the 17th century and now the cathedral of the island. The distinctive lattice-

Baltiza outer harbour looking towards the light house.

The distinctive lattice-work tower of Aghios Nikolaos on Spetsai.

work tower looks over a pebble mosaic square and the place has a wonderful peace to it, partly because the roads leading to it are stepped and inaccessible to gharries and motorbikes. Inside is a cell where the body of Paul Bonaparte, brother of Napoleon, was kept pickled in a barrel of rum for five years after he was accidentally shot on board a British ship. The road towards the Dapia from the cathedral square is a pleasant way to get into town with views of the sea glimpsed across courtyards and lush gardens.

Dapia

The centre of town where the ferries and hydrofoils berth on the long pier. A yacht should not attempt to go on the ferry pier or use the small harbour at the root of the pier which is exclusively for *caique* ferries and water-taxis. To the west of the ferry pier is a short mole where a yacht can go stern or bows-to if you decide to berth close to the town. Alternatively a yacht can anchor off to the west of the mole. Protection here is less than adequate and there is always a surge with the prevailing southeasterly wind making it extremely uncomfortable and on the mole you risk damaging your boat. The mole and the anchorage are open to the north.

The small caique harbour under the Dapia.

Ormos Zoyioryia

The large bay on the northwest end of Spetsai. There is good protection from the prevailing southeasterly winds in the bay and in the summer it is popular. Anchor where convenient in 3-10 metres on sand, weed and some rocks, good holding. Some yachts take a long line ashore on the east side. If a northerly blows in the night the bay can become untenable. Taverna/bar ashore in the summer.

On the west side of the bay is Lazaretto Cove where there is also good shelter. Anchor and take a long line ashore. Here there is better shelter from northerlies blowing down out of the Argolic. Taverna/bar ashore.

Zoyioryia is an attractive spot with a scrappy beach shaded by pine down to the waters edge. There used to be the wreck of a fairly large yacht here which according to the locals had belonged or been seized by the Commandant in charge of a German garrison on the island in World War II.

Petrokaravo

Off the northwest tip of Spetsai is the rocky islet of Petrokaravo connected intermittently with Spetsai by above and below water rocks. The islet is unmistakable and crowned by a light structure which is also prominent. There is a deep water passage (there are actually three but I will mention only one) between the reef lying approximately 300 metres off Ak Broumoboulo and the rock just above water with a reef around it lying approximately 500 metres south of Petrokaravo. Care is needed and you should have someone up front conning you through. If in doubt go around Petrokaravo.

Petrokaravo off the northwest tip of Spetsai.

Ormos Ay Paraskevi

A cove on the west side of Spetsai just over a mile SE from Ak Broumboulo. In calm weather or light southeasterlies a yacht can anchor off here, but with strong southerlies it becomes untenable when a swell is pushed in. On the southern slopes is the Villa Yasemia that figures so prominently in John Fowles' *The Magus*.

Ormos Ay Anaryiroi

The bay immediately south of Ay Paraskevi. In calm weather or light southeasterlies a yacht can anchor off here but like Paraskevi it becomes untenable in strong southerlies. It is popular in the summer with a lot of watersports activity and consequently is well supplied with tavernas and bars ashore.

On the north side of the bay is Bekeris' Cave which, so it is said, was used by smugglers to hide from the authorities. It can be reached by a path along the beach but formerly it was said that it could only be reached by swimming underwater and emerging into it that way.

Ormos Ay Petros

The long sandy bay on the south of Spetsai. In calm weather a yacht can anchor off here but with the prevailing southerlies it becomes untenable. It is also popular in the summer.

Stenon Spetsopoula

The narrow channel between Spetsai and the small island of Spetsopoula lying off its south-east tip. It is less than half a mile across and bordered by shoal water and reefs. Care is needed of the reef and shoal water off the narrow headland off Spetsai and the reef, Ifalos Papakhristou, lying to the east of it. The latter can be difficult to see with any chop on the water. Care is also needed of a large mooring buoy (unlit) slightly to the south of the fairway.

Nisis Spetsopoula

This small island is the very private property of Stavros Niarchos, the richest Greek ship owner (Onasis not excepted) around. It has a small harbour on the northern end which you can go and look at from a distance but cannot of course enter. Ashore there is a large villa set in manicured park land. Workers from Spetsai are ferried over daily.

You will often see one or other of Niarchos" yachts (read little ships) moored off the island though sadly the wonderful black three-masted schooner *Creole* has long been sold. This essay in grace and power sculpted by Camper and Nicholson in the 1930's was acquired by Niarchos when he was in the habit of competing with Onasis for status and media attention. It is said that the only question he asked before buying it was "does anyone else have one like it?" and when the answer was "no" he bought it. In its later years under Niarchos' ownership it sat sadly neglected in Zea Marina, slowly rotting away until it was bought by a Danish Sailing School.

Old cannon used for a mooring bollard on Spetsai.

CHAPTER 4

THE ARGOLIC GULF

And The Eastern Peloponnese

	Shelter	Mooring	Fuel	Water	Provisions	Tavernas	Plan
Ormos Ververoudha	C	C	O	O	O	O	
Korakonisia	B	C	O	O	O	O	
Ormos Panayitsa	C	C	O	O	O	O	
Ormos Ay Spiridon	C	C	O	O	O	O	
Koiladhia	A	AC	B	B	C	C	▪
Ormos Vourlia	O	C	O	O	O	O	
Iria harbour	B	A	O	O	O	C	
Paralion Iria	C	C	O	O	O	C	
Nisis Platia	C	C	O	O	O	O	
Khaidhari	A	AC	O	B	C	B	▪
Tolon	C	C	O	O	B	B	▪
Ormos Karathona	B	C	O	O	O	C	
Navplion	B	AB	B	A	A	A	▪
Kiverion	O	C	O	O	C	C	
Vitinia	B	AB	O	O	O	O	
Astrous	A	A	O	A	B	B	▪
Ormos Ay Dhimitrios	O	C	O	O	O	O	
Ormos Krioneri	C	C	O	O	O	O	
Ormos Zaritsi	O	C	O	O	O	O	
Tiros	B	A	B	B	C	C	▪
Leonidhion	B	A	O	A	C	C	▪
Poulithra	B	A	O	O	C	C	▪
Ormos Fokianos	C	C	O	O	O	O	▪
Kiparissi	B	AC	O	B	C	C	▪
Ieraka	A	AC	O	O	C	C	▪

	Shelter	Mooring	Fuel	Water	Provisions	Tavernas	Plan
Ormos Kremmidhi	C	C	O	O	O	O	▪
Ormos Palaio	C	C	O	O	O	O	▪
Monemvasia	C(A)	AC	B	B	B	B	▪
Ay Fokas	O	C	O	O	O	O	

Astrous

Kiparissi. The quay under the chapel in the southwest of the bay.

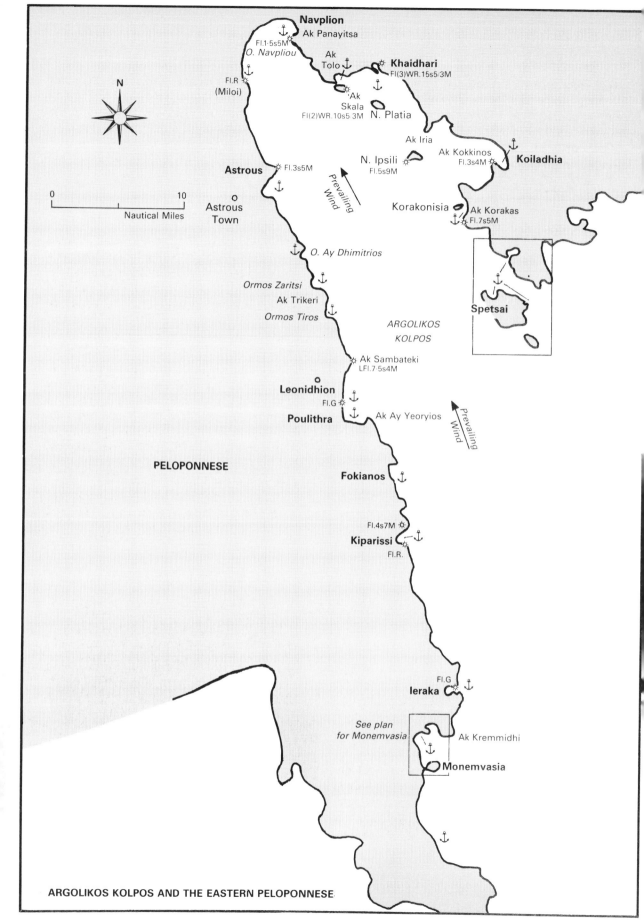

ARGOLIKOS KOLPOS AND THE EASTERN PELOPONNESE

This chapter covers Argolikos Kolpos, the gulf curving back northwards from Spetsai and Porto Kheli, and the eastern coast of the Peloponnese running from the head of the gulf right down to Ak Maleas. Compared to the Saronic islands it is comparatively little visited by yachts with most of the Athens-based yachts stopping at Idhra and Spetsai, at least for their weekend jaunts, and hardly ever venturing up into Argolikos Kolpos. There is no good reason for this and both the sailing and the scenery are magnificent with the prevailing winds in the Argolic filling in like clockwork every day and dying down at night to peaceful evenings. Further down the eastern Peloponnese things are not so ordered wind-wise, but the imposing mountains bordering the coast and the magic and interest of the places along the way more than make up for this.

On the plain of Argos at the head of Argolikos Kolpos and surveying some of the only flat land in this area is Mycenae and the triangle of other ancient cities around it - Tiryns, Argos and Asine. From this power base the Myceneans conquered most of what is now Greece and spread into Asia Minor - indeed the Trojan War is seen as an attempt by the Myceneans to spread up into the Black Sea area. The Myceneans are the Acheaens of Homer's *Iliad* and *Odyssey* and Agamemnon was most likely the King of Mycenae. The associations are powerful and vivid though strangely the landscape is not and it is the man-made artefacts rather than the setting which impresses one.

Around the eastern Peloponnese there are not many ancient associations at all, at least not on the coast. Sparta is so far inland from the coast it does not touch it and the few ancient ruins on the coast appear to have been minor settlements.

It was in the Middle Ages that the architectural monument crowning Monemvasia was built, fortified by the Byzantines and added to by the Venetians and Turks. It exemplifies what this coast once was, an obstacle to the ancient Greeks who preferred to tramp through its rugged interior and a trade route for the Byzantines and Venetians who kept to the coast and spurned the interior (with the notable and unique example of Mistra). At least for the yachtsman with a more handy vessel than his Medieval cousins and an "iron mainsail" as well the coast is not quite as forbidding as it must once have been - though it still pays to treat it with respect.

Prevailing Winds

In Argolikos Kolpos the normal summer wind blows up the gulf from the southeast. This is a thermal sea breeze and it normally arrives like clockwork around midday and blows until the sun sets. It is normally Force 4-5, occasionally slightly more, and can be relied upon from June until September. Occasionally a strong *meltemi* will get over the hump of the Argolid and blow down the gulf, though rarely more than Force 4-5. In the morning there is usually a calm or a very light northerly land breeze. Occasionally a katabatic wind will blow down off the mountains at night from the northwest and will sometimes get up to a Force 7 or so. Astrous appears to be the worst spot for this but fortunately it doesn't happen often.

From Kiparissi down to Ak Maleas there may be a sea breeze from the east to southeast though normally it is less than Force 4-5.

Monemvasia. House in the lower town.

Alternatively the *meltemi* may blow from the northeast and though it is normally Force 4-5, at times in summer it will get up to Force 7. With a strong *meltemi* big seas are pushed onto the coast and there can be severe gusts around Palaio Monemvasia.

Ormos Ververoudha

The large bay backing onto the fish lagoon at Porto Kheli. A yacht can anchor off here in 5-10 metres on mud and weed. In light southeasterlies the shelter is adequate but with strong southeasterlies a swell is pushed around the corner into the bay. Northerlies also send a swell in.

On the northern side of the bay and along to Ak Korakas are several coves which can be used in calm weather. Care is needed of reefs and rocks bordering the coast in places.

Korakonisia

Immediately around the corner from Ak Korakas is the islet of Korakonisia sheltering a cove behind it. Enter from the northwest and anchor where convenient. Good shelter from the prevailing southeasterlies and it is possible to overnight here, though if a strong northerly blows down you may have to leave.

There is translucent turquoise water everywhere and although the solitude has been broken by the large villa built on the slopes above, it is still a wonderful place. The name means islet of the ravens but there seem to be few of them around anymore.

Ormos Panayitsa

A large bay immediately southwest of Ak Ay Spiridon. There is a church on the shore and a chapel on Ak Ay Spiridon. Care needs to be taken of a rocky shelf fringing the beach. Anchor in 5-10 metres on sand with some rock. Good shelter from the prevailing southeasterlies

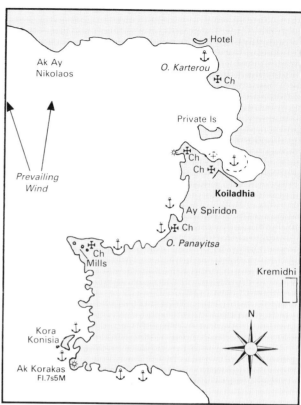

AK KORAKAS TO AK AY NIKOLAOS

although a swell sometimes creeps around the cape into the bay. Open to the north. Clear water and a beach ashore.

Ormos Ay Spiridon

The bay immediately northeast of Ak Ay Spiridon. Anchor in 4-8 metres on sand and some rock. Better shelter than Panayitsa.

Koiladhia

An anchorage and fishing harbour tucked into the bay around Ak Kokkinos (Red Cape).

Pilotage

Approach A chapel on Ak Kokkinos and the large cathedral in the village are conspicuous. The entrance between Ak Kokkinos and Nisis Koiladhia will not be seen from the southwest until you are close to it. Care needs to be taken of the reef running out from Ak

Looking out to the south side of the entrance to Koiladhia.

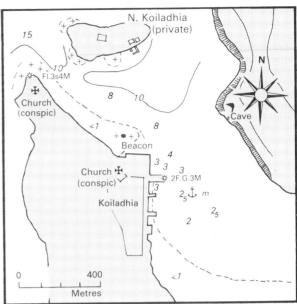

KOILADHIA
37°25'N 23°07'·7E (2F.G.3M)

Kokkinos and the final approach should be from the northwest. In the channel under Nisis Koiladhia care is needed of the reef and shoal water fringing the coast with a reef marked by a beacon just northwest of the quay. Entrance can also be made between the east side of Nisis Koiladhia and the coast.

Mooring Anchor off in 2.5-4 metres where convenient. Care needs to be taken of numerous permanent moorings in the bay. The bottom is sticky mud, excellent holding. Good all-round shelter. It is possible to go stern or bows-to or alongside one of the piers off the village but these are usually occupied by fishing boats and the prevailing southeasterly tends to set up a small swell across the bay making it uncomfortable until the wind drops at night.

Facilities

Services Water on the quay and a mini-tanker can deliver fuel by arrangement.

Provisions Most provisions can be found in the village. Ice available.

Eating Out Several tavernas on the waterfront which may have fresh fish off the boats.

Other PO. OTE. Taxi.

General

The village would win no architectural prizes for its "pour-and-fill" buildings but it more than makes up for this with friendly inhabitants and a proper working atmosphere serving the large fishing fleet based here (*caiques* are built ashore) and the agricultural hinterland. It is unlikely to attract tourists as the water is muddied by silt whipped up from the bottom so it is not the translucent blue expected in the Mediterranean. It has attracted a Greek shipping millionaire who owns the islet of Koiladhia in the entrance. A large house has been built on the islet and there is a small harbour where the owner berths his motor yacht - needless to say you cannot berth here unless invited.

Koiladhia looking from the south end of the bay.

Pausanias mentions an ancient city called Mazes in the vicinity which was probably here at Koiladhia although nothing now remains. In fact the area has much older associations in the Francithi Cave prominent in the cliffs opposite the village where numerous prehistoric remains have been found. Apart from the bones of various animals, the skeleton of a stone-age man from the Mesolithic period was found, the oldest inhabitant of Greece so far discovered and a find important for the piecing together of early Neolithic life in Europe.

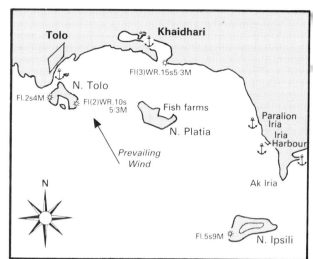

AK IRIA TO TOLO

The Francithi Cave opposite Koiladhia where the skeleton from the Mesolithic era was found

Ormos Karterou

The bay just above Ormos Koiladhia. A hotel is prominent on the slopes. In calm weather or light southeasterlies a yacht can anchor off the beach, but with strong southeasterlies a swell is pushed into the bay.

Ormos Vourlia

A large bay opposite Nisis Ipsili. In calm weather a yacht can anchor off in here although it is everywhere very deep. On the west side there is an inlet just northeast of Ak Iria which looks worth exploring

Nisis Ipsili

A high bold dome-shaped island dropping straight down into the sea. There are considerable depths everywhere around it with nowhere to anchor off. The inscription "ruin" on the chart looks intriguing.

Iria Harbour

Just over a mile NNW of Ak Iria is a small fishing harbour. The houses of Paralion Iria will be seen and closer in the breakwater sheltering the harbour. An L-shaped breakwater with a snub breakwater at the entrance faces northwest. There are 2-3 metre depths at the entrance and 1-2 metre depths inside. Care is needed of floating mooring lines used by the fishing boats. A small yacht can just squeeze in and berth with a long line to the breakwater near the entrance. Shelter is reasonable from the prevailing southeasterly wind.

A short walk away at Paralion Iria there is a taverna/bar on the beach. Here in a 5-10 metre patch yachts sometimes anchor off although with a fresh southeasterly a swell is pushed down onto the anchorage and it is most uncomfortable.

Nisis Platia

The low island lying off Ormos Valtou. It used to be possible to anchor off the north side of the island but a fish farm now obstructs most of this anchorage and does little for the former charm and solitude of the place.

Khaidhari quay looking from the anchorage.

Khaidhari

The deep slit of an inlet on the coast opposite Nisis Platia.

Pilotage

Approach The entrance is difficult to make out from the distance although the cleft in the cliffs can be identified with a fair degree of certainty. Closer in the ruins of a small fort on the western side of the entrance and the light structure and a small stone hut on the eastern side will be seen. The entrance is deep and clear of dangers and entry is straightforward. Once into the bay care is needed of the fish farm on the south side.

Mooring Anchor off in 6-12 metres taking care of the permanent moorings or go stern or bows-to either side of the outer end of the new pier on the north side. The bottom is mud and weed, good holding. Shelter is all-round

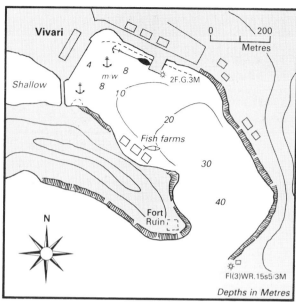

KHAIDHARI
37°31'·4N 22°56'·1E (Fl(3)WR.5/3M)

The Venetian mini-fort on the western side of the entrance to Khaidhari. It fell a year after its construction in 1714.

in the inlet but a slight swell penetrates with the prevailing southeasterlies which makes a berth on the quay slightly uncomfortable.

Facilities
Services Water in the village.
Provisions Most provisions can be found in the village.
Eating Out Several tavernas on the waterfront.
Other Metered telephone. Taxi.

General
The fjord-like inlet is magnificent with high land and cliffs rising sheer from the water except at the head where a barrage separates the inlet from a lagoon used as a fish farm. The human habitation is not magnificent with uninspired square concrete buildings of recent vintage. Not that I want to damn the place but I like it so much that I wish the locals had expended a bit more imagination in their building efforts

On the western entrance point are the remains of a small fort which is probably of Venetian origin. The Venetians thought the harbour would have been a useful one for a fleet anchorage and in 1714 built the little fort to guard the entrance. They also built shipyards at the head of the bay to haul and repair their naval fleet. One year later Pasha Khodja arrived with a fleet of 150 ships and destroyed the fort and seven ships hauled out in the yard. This push by the Turks was to drive the Venetians out of the Peloponnese for good though they still retained other footholds in Greece.

Tolon

A resort lying at the western end of the long sandy beach running around from near Khaidhari and partially sheltered by Nisis Tolo.

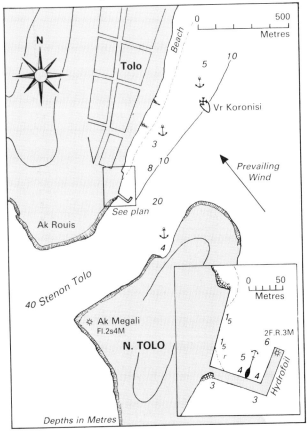

TOLO
37°30'·9N 22°51'·5W (2F.R.3M)

Tolon looking from the anchorage.

Pilotage

Approach From the east and west the buildings of Tolon are easily identified but from the south Nisis Tolo obscures the view. However the general location is easy enough to determine from the relative position of Nisis Platia. Closer in the channel between Nisis Tolo and the village will be seen. Ifalos Tolo, a reef lying just under a mile SSE of the southeast of Ak Skala on Nisis Tolo has a least depth over it of 3.7 metres so will only be of concern to deep draught craft.

Mooring Anchor off the beach in 5-10 metres. Care is needed of the numerous permanent moorings on the bottom. The bottom is sand, good holding. The shelter here is better than it looks as the prevailing southeasterlies do not blow home and although some swell is pushed in, it dies down at night. The small harbour is crowded with local boats and generally they do not like visiting yachts in here.

Facilities

Services Water and fuel in the town only.

Provisions Good shopping for all provisions in the town.

Eating Out Numerous tavernas on the waterfront and in the town.

Other PO. OTE. Bank. Hire motorbikes and cars. Intermittent bus to Navplion. Hydrofoil to Piraeus.

General

What was once a small fishing village has expanded and expanded as a tourist resort on the strength of the fine sandy beach stretching around the coast. Hotels and condominiums now line the beach catering for the package holidays that Tolon figures in. It is not my sort of place, too mercenary by half, and there is little to keep the visitor here apart from the plethora of tavernas.

Just north of Tolon is ancient Asine which was an important city early on, but declined after it was sacked by the Argives. The inhabitants had sided with Sparta and after their allies left the Argives attacked it. When it was apparent that all was lost the Asinians packed up their women and children and chattels into their boats and sailed off to settle in the Gulf of Messinia in the Peloponnese closer to the Spartans. You can identify the coastal site as you sail up the coast to Navplion and really this

Nisis Tolo looking out from the harbour.

is the best way to see it as there is little left of the ancient city and only dedicated ruin-hounds should go by land.

Nisis Tolo

The island lying off Tolon has several anchorages which can be used in calm weather.

Channel Anchorage. Anchor off in the bight at the island end of the shallowish (8 metres least depth in the fairway) strip of water joining the island to Tolon. Some protection from southeasterlies.

Nisis Dhaskalia. With care of the reefs a yacht can anchor in the bay under Nisis Dhaskalia, the islet on the south side of Nisis Tolo. A swell is pushed in by the prevailing southeasterlies.

Ormos Karathona

The large bay on the north side of Ak Khondros. A breakwater has been built out from the southern entrance point nearly to the tiny islet in the bay. Anchor in 2.5-6 metres on the south side of the bay. The bottom is sand, mud and weed, good holding. Good shelter from the prevailing winds and under the breakwater there is nearly all-round shelter.

Ashore several tavernas open in the summer. The bay is an attractive pace with steep rocky slopes above the tree-lined beach and is popular with Navplionites in the summer.

Navplion

The largest town in the gulf and the commercial harbour for the hinterland.

Pilotage

Approach The town hidden by a low ridge will not be seen from the south. A chapel on Ak Khondros is easily identified and a large hotel on the saddle of the ridge is conspicuous. The fortress of Palamidhi is also conspicuous though not as much as might be expected because the honey coloured stone blends with the rock of the mountain. Closer in Nisis Bourtzi with a fort on it and the light structure

on Akronavplia are easily identified. Once up to Akronavplia things are straightforward. Care is occasionally needed of cargo ships entering and leaving.

Mooring Go alongside or stern or bows-to the east quay or on the west side of the stubby pier. The bottom is sticky mud and good holding. Good shelter from the prevailing southeasterlies although dust off the quay is blown across your decks. Sometimes at night a northwesterly will blow though it is normally more uncomfortable than dangerous. The east quay is very smelly with sewerage emptying into it and berths on the west side of the pier only marginally less so. Navplion is a port of entry and the port police will come down to see you.

Facilities

Services Water on the quay when you can find the waterman. Fuel can be delivered by mini-tanker.

Provisions Good shopping for all provisions in the town although most shops are off to the east.

Eating Out Numerous tavernas of all types and numerous bars along the waterfront. Prices in Navplion are on a par with those in Athens and the reason for this, the man in the puppet-shop suggested, is because most of them are summer only affairs run by Athenians.

Approach to Navplion showing the light structure on Akronauplia and Nisis Bourtzi.

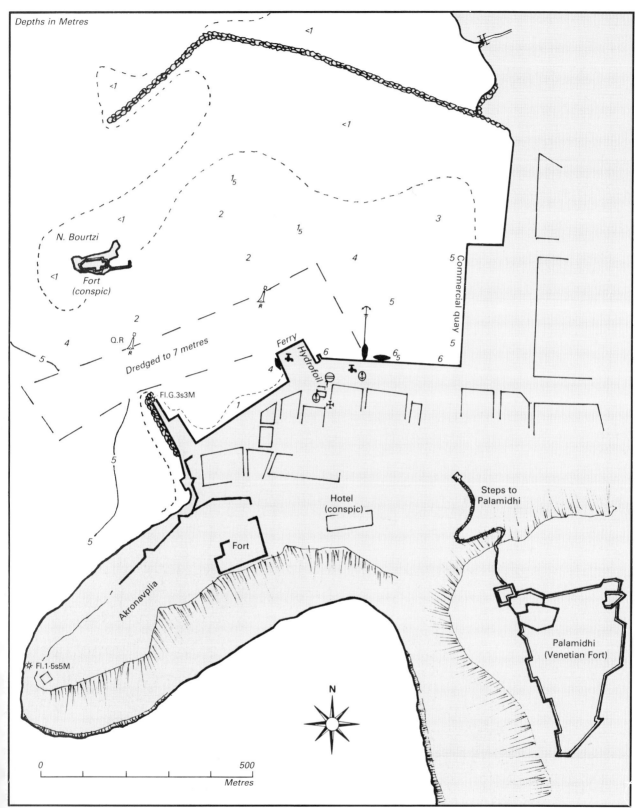

Depths in Metres

<1

<1

<1

1_5

2

3

N. Bourtzi

<1

Fort
(conspic)

2

1_5

2

4

5

Commercial quay

5

Q.R

4

5

Dredged to 7 metres

Ferry

6

6_5

6

Hydrofoil

4

5

Fl.G.3s3M

1

Steps to
Palamidhi

Hotel
(conspic)

Fort

Palamidhi
(Venetian Fort)

Akronavplia

Fl.1·5s5M

N

0

500

Metres

NAVPLION 37°34'·1N 22°47'·6E (Fl.G)

142

Other PO. OTE. Banks. Doctors. Dentist. Hire motorbikes and cars. Bus to Athens. Hydrofoil to Piraeus and stops along the way.

General

It is a great pity the harbour is so smelly. The old town is an enchanting place with a mixture of Venetian, Turkish and neo-classical buildings from the early 19th century when Navplion was briefly capital of the newly liberated Greece. Buildings lean out at odd angles, wooden Turkish balconies perch over the streets, and then suddenly you come on the central square with the old Venetian arsenal, now a museum, imposing at the western end. Bougainvillaea and clematis grow everywhere concealing whole walls and covering ruins. An old Turkish fountain still runs. A Venetian lion grins inanely. Navplion has charm and lots of it.

The town was quite probably a Mycenean naval base though nothing remains. It's mythopaeic founder was Nauplius, a son of Poseidon. His son Palamedes gives his name to the steep rock behind the town and also to the Venetian citadel on top. Palamedes is credited with a whole range of inventions including the lighthouse, most of the Greek alphabet, weights and measures and the games of chess and dice - a busy man or god. The original Greek town was conquered and razed by Damocrates of Argos in 676 BC and never recovered. It doesn't enter the history books again until 589 AD when it is recorded as part of Byzantine territory. Its fortunes were to be an up-and-down affair thereafter with successive occupation by the Franks, Venetians, Turks, and finally the Greeks in 1822.

Looking out to Nisis Bourtzi from Navplion town quay.

Looking up to Palamidhi from Navplion town.

The fortress on top of Palamidhi was built by the Venetians in three years from 1711 to 1714. Despite the thick walls, the successive defensive walls, and the impregnable looking position on its sheer rocky site, the fort fell after only eight days siege by the Turks just one year after it was completed. The fortress served the Turks little better. The Turkish garrison in the fort surrendered it without a shot being fired when the doughty Boubalina sailed up here and threatened the Turkish fleet with fire ships - one can only imagine this woman put the fear of Allah in the poor old Turks.

It can be reached by 857 steps from the town (take a bottle of water) or the indolent can be driven up to the summit via the new road to the east. The views from the top, as you might expect, are stupendous and in places those who suffer from vertigo will be troubled when walking around the summit.

The other fortress at Navplion, somewhat overshadowed by the bulk of Palamidhi, is on the steep-sided headland sticking out to the west from Navplion town. Akronavplia was the site of the ancient Greek acropolis and of subsequent castles built by the Byzantines, added to by the Franks, and also by the Venetians who built the evocatively named Castel del Toro.

Navplion was the capital of Greece from 1828 to 1834 when Otto of Bavaria moved the capital to Athens. Ioannou Capodistriou, the first president of Greece, installed himself at Navplion and bestowed some of the fine neo-classical buildings on the city. He had to cope with much dissension and rebellion amongst the various guerrilla chiefs who had fought the war and he was finally to fail in his diplomacy and pay with his life. In 1831 Capodistriou was assassinated by rebels from the Mani led by Kolkotronas in front of the Church of Ayios Spiridon. Kolkotronas was later imprisoned in Palamidhi. Otto of Bavaria was chosen as his successor and in 1834 moved the capital to Athens. Some idea of the anarchy which prevailed within the infant democracy is given in Julia Ward Howe's account from the mid 19th century.

"The evening of our sojourn in Argos saw an excitement much like that which blocked the street at Nauplia. The occasion was the same - the bringing home of a brigand's head; but this the very head and fount of all the brigands, Kitzos himself, upon whose very head had been set a price of several thousand drachmas. Our veteran with difficulty obtained a view of the same, and reported accordingly. The robber chief of Edmond About's "Hadji Stauros", had been shot while sighting at his gun. He had fallen with one eye shut and one open, and in this form of feature his disseevered head remained. The soldier who was its fortunate captor carried it concealed in a bag, with its long elf-locks lying loose about it. He showed it with some unwillingness, fearing to have the

prize wrested from him. It was, however, taken on board of our steamer, and carried to Athens, there to be identified and buried."
Julia Ward Howe *From the Oak to the Olive* 1868

With the death of the brigand Julia Howe was able to proceed on to Mycenae, a journey which had been advised against while the brigand Kitzos was in the area. Today the only brigands around are confined to the bars in Navplion. Navplion is of course the logical place to make excursions to Tiryns and Mycenae. Coach trips with a guide are organised in the summer or you can take a taxi or hire a car or a motorbike. Do remember to take stout footwear, a hat, and a bottle of water - it gets warm at Mycenae in the height of summer.

Tiryns

Although not as well known as Mycenae, the ruins of Tiryns are impressive and worth a look at. The walled city sits on a low rocky outcrop with inner passages and storerooms. Pausanias compared the site with the Egyptian pyramids and certainly the size of the building materials ensured much of it could not be carted away for other buildings. Some of the rocks used in the construction weigh as much as 30 tons and some of the walls are nearly 10 metres thick - it makes the construction at Mycenae look flimsy by comparison.

The city is said to have been founded by Proitos of Argos who enlisted the Cyclops of Lykia to help him build it. Amongst the descendants of Proitis was Eurystheseus who is credited with giving Heracles (Hercules) his twelve labours and probably also for the popularity of the cult of Heracles which swept the Argolid and persisted for centuries. Heracles to my mind has always been the archetypal "kick-sand-in-your-face" sort of strongman, capable of astounding feats of strength but a little slow on the uptake and subject to all the duplicity going - so much so you have to sympathise with him in the end.

Tiryns has been inhabited from around the third millennium BC and continued to be inhabited right up to the Mycenean period when further walls were added and a palace built. It was inhabited after the demise of the Myceneans and around the 8th century BC a Temple to Hera was built. The city was subjugated by the Argives in 486 BC and effectively the site was abandoned.

Looking over to the Peloponnese from Palamidhi. Vertigo sufferers beware.

Mycenae

This is the city and the site that has given its name to the warrior race that subjugated much of Greece and provided the material for Homer's Acheaens. It is probably (and if not it should be) the city of Agamemnon and the gold death mask found in a burial tomb is popularly said to be his. Perhaps from here the heroics and the pathos of the Trojan War captured in the *Iliad* and the *Odyssey* were set in motion when Agamemnon declared his intention to avenge the wrongs of Paris and bring Helen back from Troy. And underneath all this is the brooding horror of the tragedy of the House of Atreus.

The Lion Gate at Mycenae.

The tale begins with Tantalus, son of Zeus, who for some benighted reason served up his son Pelops as a gift for the gods. Not surprisingly they were horrified and reconstituted poor Pelops complete with an ivory shoulder because the goddess Demeter had inadvertently eaten it. Pelops settled in the "island" now named after him, the Peloponnese (Peloponnisos). Tantalus was sent off to Hades where he was forever to be tormented by hunger and thirst.

The descendants of Tantalus were blighted with a curse for his foul deed. Pelops had two sons, Thyestes and Atreus, and when Thyestes seduced Atreus' wife he had the children of Thyestes killed and cut up to be served to their father for dinner. It doesn't end here. The progeny of Atreus included Agamemnon and Menelaus, husband of Helen (later of Troy). To appease the gods and help the campaign Agamemnon sacrificed his daughter Iphigenia. While he was away Agamemnon's wife Klytemistra had taken a lover and along the way Agamemnon had picked up a lover of his own, Cassandra. Cassandra predicted horror and blood and so it was when Klytemistra killed her husband Agamemnon.

I know it is convoluted but after all I have tried to condense what Aeschylus packed into his dramatic trilogy, the *Orestria*. Why it is called the *Orestria* will become clear when you realise the horror is not over. Orestes was Klytemistra's son and urged on by his sister Elektra, he returned to kill his mother to avenge his father's death. He performed the deed unwillingly and afterwards suffered such remorse that the goddess Athena forgave him and lifted the curse from the House of Atreus.

I can be forgiven for dwelling on this story, (which I find fascinating and perhaps indicative of the bloody and back-stabbing era of Mycenae), if I do not dwell on the site itself. The plan is self explanatory and there are detailed texts available to explain the successive layers of building and rebuilding. Like Tiryns it is the scale of the building, the walls up to 8 metres thick and the blocks of stone weighing up to 20 tons that are impressive. There are the

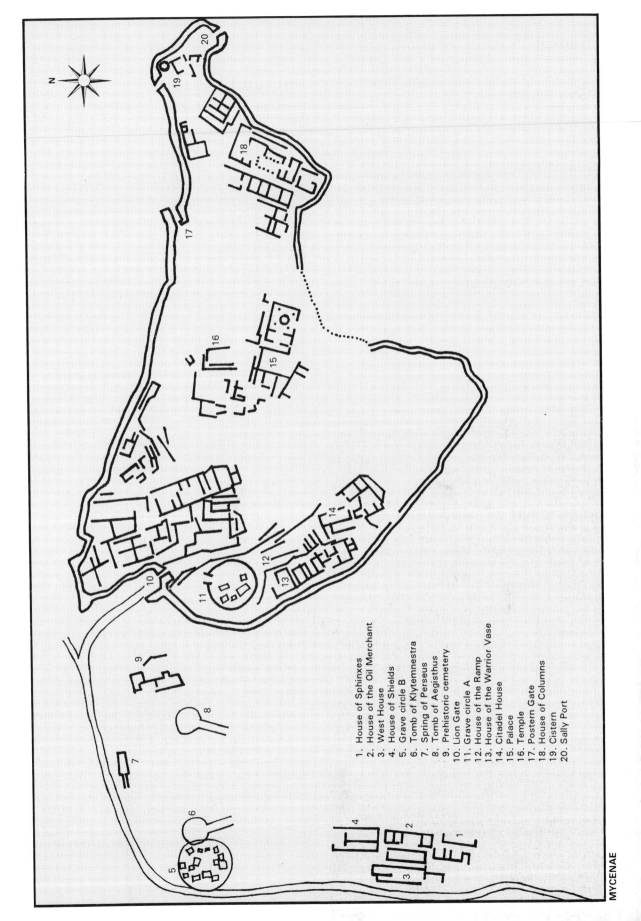

1. House of Sphinxes
2. House of the Oil Merchant
3. West House
4. House of Shields
5. Grave circle B
6. Tomb of Klytemnestra
7. Spring of Perseus
8. Tomb of Aegisthus
9. Prehistoric cemetery
10. Lion Gate
11. Grave circle A
12. House of the Ramp
13. House of the Warrior Vase
14. Citadel House
15. Palace
16. Temple
17. Postern Gate
18. House of Columns
19. Cistern
20. Sally Port

MYCENAE

tombs where Schleimann found the burial remains and numerous gold objects including the mask of Agamemnon, the site of the royal palace, and tunnels and storage rooms.

The city reached its zenith in the 13th century BC and declined abruptly with the Mycenean empire in the 11th century BC for no good reason that anyone has come up. Perhaps plague or some other disease, an unknown warrior race (perhaps the mysterious "sea people"), a natural disaster like a massive earthquake, or perhaps just a decline in the leadership and fortunes of the warrior race (they may have become fat and lazy with soft living), suddenly terminated an empire.

In the museum in Navplion (in the old Venetian arsenal in the square) there is a Mycenean suit of armour and this more than anything else has shaped my ideas of what a Mycenean looked like. The armour and the boars tusk helmet look like something out my boyhood books with illustrations of the Saracens and seems strangely contemporary for the 2nd millennium BC. Add to the images the armour conjures up the thin cruel lips and hard features of Agamemnon's death mask and add to that the horrors of the curse on the House of Atreus and it can all send a chill down your spine that needs a brief spell sitting on the sun-warmed rock of Mycenae to dispel. It is evidently a common emotion once acquainted with the tragedy of the House of Atreus and Mycenae.

"Orestes, running out of the back door
Felt the wall's shadow lighten on his back,
Where blood and milk, mingled, seeped on the floor.

He looked one last time on that town the sack
Of Troy made famous, then forgot, and ran.
Free in the hills, no one could fetch him back.

"I am alone, free from the ties of men:
Odysseus drifts among the bladder wrack,
And swift Achilles lies as still as stone.

Behind the summit now my trodden track."
That year the blood-red poppies did not bloom.

The land seemed dead, the rocks of Lethe cracked.

"And I was glad to see the Furies come".
At Mycenae Richard Stoneman

Kiverion

A small village on the west side of Argolikos Kolpos approximately 3½ miles southwest of Navplion. The cluster of houses of the village are easily identified. In the morning calm or in light southeasterlies you can anchor tucked into the bight off the village. Its a good place for a lunch stop but the normal southeasterlies blowing up the gulf make it unsuitable for an overnight stop. Tavernas ashore.

Vitinia

Off the factory immediately north of the village there is a small harbour that a few fishing boats use. Most of the quayed area is for commercial use.

Astrous

A fishing village and small resort tucked under a headland southwest of Tolon.

Pilotage

Approach From the north and south the headland under which the harbour is tucked looks like an island. From the south the houses of the village and a few hotels around the beach are easily identified. From the north and east the houses of the village will not be seen until around the headland. The castle on the summit of the headland will be seen when closer in and the outer breakwater is easily identified. Entry is straightforward once up to the breakwater.

Mooring Go stern or bows-to the south mole where convenient. It is better to go bows-to as underwater ballasting extends out a short distance in most places though it is generally deeper than it looks close to the quay. Care is also needed of the floating lines of permanent

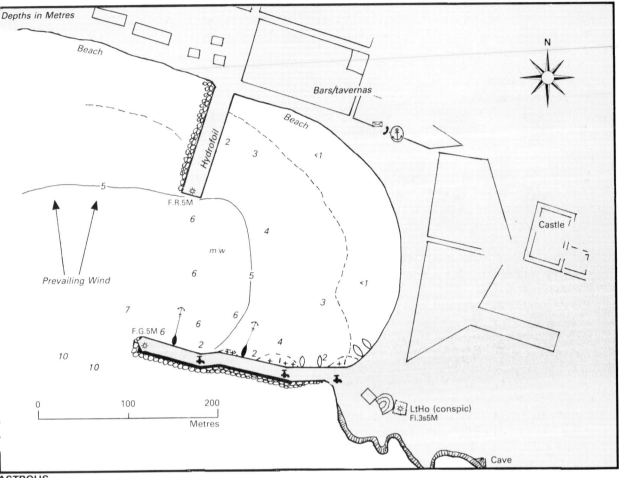

ASTROUS
37°24'·9N 22°46'·1E (F.G.5M)

moorings. The bottom is mud and weed, generally good holding although there seem to be patches where the holding is indifferent. Good shelter from the prevailing wind and nearly all-round shelter. Occasionally at night a katabatic wind may blow off the mountains from the west-northwest, sometimes up to Force 7 or so though generally less, so ensure your anchor is well in. No swell of any consequence is generated by this wind but the force of the wind hits yachts beam-on on the south quay. A yacht should not go on the north quay which is used by a tripper boat and the hydrofoil.

Facilities

Services Water on the quay - the waterman will call around.

Provisions Most provisions can be found in the village.

Eating Out A good choice of tavernas. The *Elatos*, the first taverna encountered walking into the village is a bit pompous but has better than average food at reasonable prices. The *Bakxos* on the beach in the northwest corner of the harbour serves honest Greek fare with a superb view. In the village several of the tavernas often have good fresh fish. Bars on the waterfront looking over the harbour.

Other PO. OTE. Money changing facilities. Taxi. Hydrofoil to Piraeus.

Astrous harbour looking down from the castle.

General

Astrous is one of my favourite places in the gulf. Properly it is Paralion Astrous and Astrous proper is the village 4 kilometres inland. It has enough tourism for a couple of good tavernas. The harbour is clean enough to swim in or you can pop over the breakwater to a small shingle beach. The harbour offers more than adequate shelter in the summer. And there are pleasant walks up to the castle or right into Astrous proper if you fancy a walk through agricultural land and orchards. There is nothing you "should see" and plenty of lazing around to be done.

The castle above the village does not entail a lot of energy to get to and is a pleasant ruinous place to wander around. Most of what remains was built by the Venetians though originally an acropolis stood on the headland, probably further to the northeast of the castle. Astrous was established around the 13th century BC and probably takes its name from the word "asti" (city) which was then corrupted to Astri and so Astrous or Astrous. In the ruins of Astri a caryatid was discovered similar to those that adorned the Erechthyeion in Athens except this one is unique because it is the only caryatid discovered with its head intact. The Venetian castle is nothing exceptional, more homely than defensive, and local tales tell of a secret tunnel leading down to the cave by the sea though I have never discovered it or even traces of it.

Ormos Astrous

In calm weather and light southeasterlies you can anchor off the long sandy beach in the southwest corner. Here there is some protection from the prevailing southeasterlies although a swell tends to roll in.

Astrous. Castle ruins.

Ay Andreas

A hamlet 3 miles south of Astrous. There is a tiny fishing harbour here really too small for even small yachts. The village of Ay Andreas inland has been identified as ancient Brasiae and it is thought ships used to moor at the mouth of the river on the coast and may have navigated right up it to the ancient city.

Ormos Ay Dhimitrios

A bay 3 miles south of Ay Andreas under Ak Ay Dhimitrios. In calm weather a yacht can anchor in here - a good lunch stop under steep threatening slopes.

Ormos Krioneri

Another bay about a mile south of Ay Dhimitrios suitable in calm weather. Anchor on the south side of the bay.

Ormos Zaritsi

Another large bay 2 miles south of Krioneri suitable in calm weather. Anchor off the beach.

Tiros

Pilotage

Approach Three windmills on the ridge southeast of the harbour are conspicuous. Closer in the mole shows up well against the beach. From the north care is needed of the rock off the north entrance point of the bay.

Mooring Go stern or bows-to the mole leaving the outer end free for the hydrofoil. Care is needed of a rocky patch about one third of the way up from the root of the mole. In southerlies or settled weather you can also go onto the short jetty on the beach. The resident fishing boats have laid moorings so care is needed not to foul them. Good shelter from the prevailing wind. With strong north to north easterlies the harbour would be uncomfortable and may be untenable.

Facilities

Services Water in the village. Fuel can be delivered to the harbour.

Provisions Most provisions can be found in the village. Ice available.

Eating Out Tavernas on the waterfront.

Other PO. Taxis. Hydrofoil to Piraeus and points along the way.

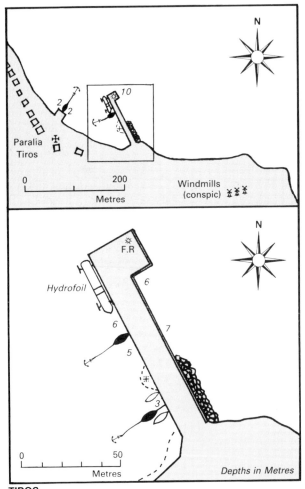

Paralia
Tiros

0   200

Metres

Windmills
(conspic)

Hydrofoil

F.R

6

6

7

5

3

0   50

Metres   *Depths in Metres*

TIROS
37°15'N 22°52'E

General

For most of the year Tiros is a sleepy little place serving the fishermen and agricultural hinterland. In the summer it benefits from a little local tourism when a few Athenian families are packed off here away from the *nefos*. The village is a most pleasant little place on the edge of a grey pebble beach with orchards behind under the rocky slopes of the Peloponnese. The main village lies a stiff walk up the hill behind. You can visit the Monastery of Elona by taxi from here and get a better nights sleep than you would at Leonidhion when the southeasterly is blowing.

Leonidhion

A small harbour at the end of the long sandy beach after Ak Sambateki.

Pilotage

Approach The harbour is difficult to identify from the distance as the beach continues along part of the breakwater and the breakwater itself blends into the rock behind. Head for the general vicinity and closer in a windmill on the beach converted to a house and a white church will be seen. Closer still the buildings of the hamlet (all stone and brown tiles designed to blend into the landscape) and the end of the breakwater will be seen. There is usually a confused swell at the entrance with the prevailing winds so care is needed turning to enter the harbour.

Leonidhion.

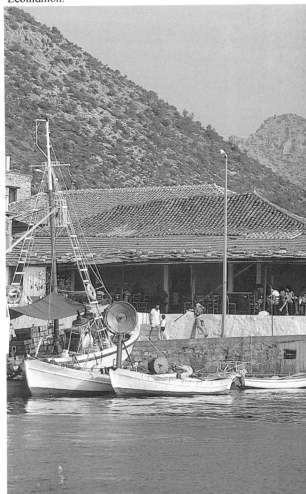

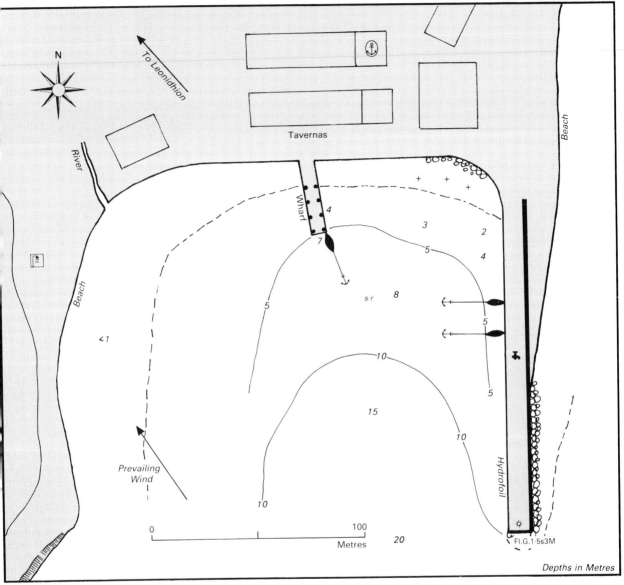

LEONIDHION
37°08ʹ·8N 22°53ʹ·6E (Fl.G.3M)

Mooring Go stern or bows-to the mole leaving the hydrofoil berth clear. The bottom is hard sand, rocks and weed, not the best holding so make sure your anchor is well in. The harbour is uncomfortable (some say torturous) with the prevailing southeasterlies which send in a swell which hits boats beam-on and sets them rolling with a sickening motion. It is safe enough with the prevailing winds - just uncomfortable. Fortunately you can escape ashore and watch the motion from a static taverna chair.

Facilities

Services Water on the quay.

Provisions Simple provisions only. There is good shopping in Leonidhion proper inland.

Eating Out Several tavernas on the waterfront which are all pretty much of a muchness serving good basic Greek fare.

Other Taxi. Hydrofoil to Piraeus.

General

The harbour and hamlet, correctly Skala Leonidhion (Skala means a ladder or staircase) sits under impressive precipitous slopes on the edge of the valley plain that extends back up to Leonidhion proper some 4 kilometres inland. It is a genial place, visited by a few back-packers and yachts, but with no established tourism yet.

Leonidhion proper is built on either side of a river (usually dry in summer) on the floor of the valley. The town is the capital of the region and it is said that the local Tsakonian dialect preserves traces of the original Doric Greek. Some of the local rugs and tapestries are also said to preserve Doric designs and motifs.

From Leonidhion or Skala you can take a taxi to the Monastery of Elona tucked into a cliff side eyrie, though the drive up to the monastery with a local driver is more scary than standing on the edge of the monastery parapet looking down the cliff.

Leonidhion.

Poulithra

A small fishing harbour 2 miles south of Leonidhion. A white church near the shore is conspicuous. The harbour is very small with room for a couple of yachts only amongst the local fishing boats. Go stern or bows-to the end of the short mole taking care of the numerous laid moorings on the bottom. Good shelter from the prevailing southeasterlies but open north.

Ashore there are numerous tavernas and some provisions can be found in the village. In the summer the village always seems full of ex-pats who return here from their chosen country to the place of their birth.

Ormos Fokianos

A large bay lying a mile south of Ak Tourkovigla. Anchor at the head of the bay off the beach. The surroundings here are magnificent and the bay is a wonderful spot, but the prevailing southeasterlies send a swell in.

Around Fokianos or a bit further south is the dividing line for the prevalence of the southeasterly sea breeze that blows up into Argolikos Kolpos. There may be either a southerly or a northerly here or a flat patch where you catch only the swell but no wind.

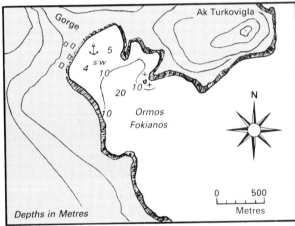

FOKIANOS
37°04′N 22°59′E

POULITHRA
37°07′N 22°54′·2E (F.R.4M)

Kiparissi · *Nigel Patten.*

Kiparissi

The large bay lying 4 miles south of Fokianos.

Pilotage

Approach The entrance to the bay is difficult to make out from the north and south. From the northeast the village will be seen. From the north there is little to identify where the bay is until the light structure on the north side is seen. From the south the rocky islet off the entrance will be seen but the light structure on the south side will not be seen until you are into the bay. The houses of the village are obvious once you are up to the entrance.

Mooring There are three possibilities depending on the wind and ground-swell.

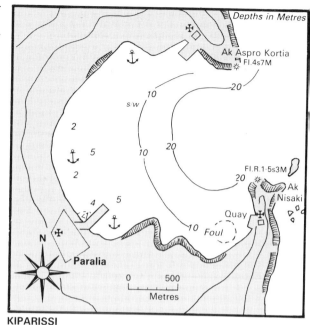

KIPARISSI
36°59'·1N 23°00'·3E (Ak Kortia light)

Kiparissi village. *Nigel Patten.*

1. Off the village in the southeast of the bay. Anchor off or go alongside the east side of the pier. With northerlies it can be uncomfortable though it only really becomes untenable in fresh or strong northerlies. You are close to all the facilities in the village here.

2. Off the chapel in the cove on the southwest side of the bay. Go stern or bows-to the quay off the chapel. There are 2-2.5 metres off the quay dropping off quickly to 15 metres a short distance off so make sure you have plenty of scope for the anchor. Alternatively anchor and take a long line ashore just southeast of the quay although care is needed of the permanent moorings on the bottom for local fishing boats. Good shelter from southerlies and northerlies send in a limited swell.

3. Anchor in the north of the bay or tuck inside the new ferry quay (being enlarged at the time of writing). This is the best place to be in northerlies though unless you can get under the new quayed area it is not a good place in strong southerlies.

Facilities
Services Water in the village.
Provisions Most provisions can be found.
Eating Out Tavernas ashore. Fresh fish is often available.
Other PO. OTE. Hydrofoil to Piraeus and south to Monemvasia.

General
The bay is quite simply majestic. Slopes rise precipitously to razor sharp spines over which thunderstorms sometimes break in the summer. If you are off the chapel in the southwest cove light the oil lamp for a little saintly intervention if the fishermen have not already done so. The mountainous setting gives a good idea of the backdrop to the coast further south - this is wild and savage country and although Sparta is a long way inland, this is the sort of country the Spartans lived and prospered in and you can see where we get the word "spartan" from.

Kiparissi. Fishing boat tucked under the quay by the chapel.

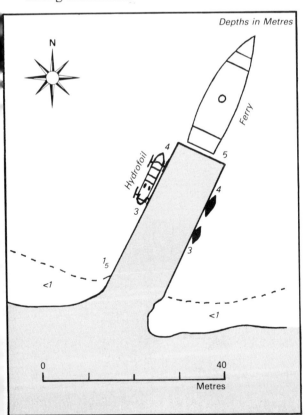

KIPARISSI TOWN QUAY

Anchorages down to Ieraka

Between Kiparissi and Ieraka there are some wild and wonderful anchorages that can be used in calm weather.

Vathi Avlaki. Under Ak Vathi Avlaki there is bay at the foot of a gorge which can be used.

Just over a mile south there is a cove which can be used although it is quite deep for anchoring.

Chapel Cove. South of this anchorage before Ak Vathi a chapel is conspicuous. In calm weather anchor in the cove underneath although again it is quite deep for anchoring.

Ieraka

A small village tucked into a rocky inlet 2 miles south of Ak Vathi.

Pilotage

Approach The crooked cleft in the cliffs that is the entrance is difficult to see even when you are quite close to it. From the north the chapel near Ak Vathi will be seen. From the south an islet, Nisis Dhaskalio, can be identified. In the entrance the light structure on the north side will eventually be seen. With strong northerlies there can be a confused swell in the entrance as the waves rebound off the rocky cliffs.

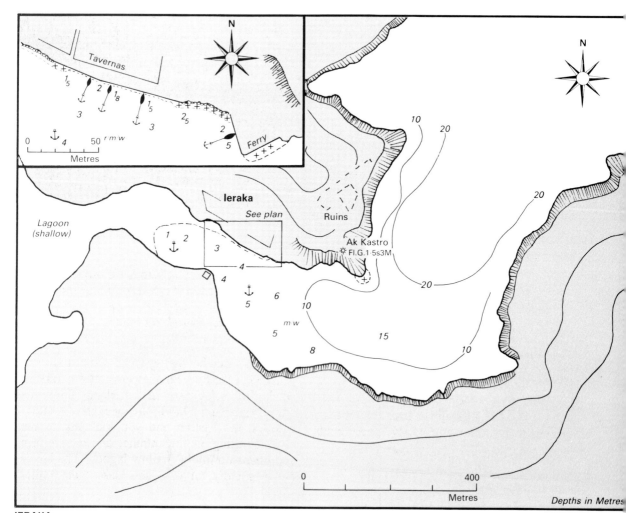

IERAKA
36°47'·2N 23°05'·3E (Ak Kastro light)

Ieraka looking from the slopes near Ak Kastri.

Mooring Once into the inlet care is needed of the section of ferry quay which has collapsed and is just underwater at the time of writing. Go bows-to the quay off the village with care as it is bordered by rocky shallows in places. Alternatively anchor off at the western end. Shallow draught craft can creep up quite a way to the west. The bottom is mud, rocks and weed, reasonable holding. Good all-round shelter inside although fresh to strong northerlies set up a surge which causes boats on the quay to roll.

Facilities
Services Water in the village.
Provisions Basic provisions can be found.

Eating Out Several tavernas on the waterfront which will often have fresh fish (and often little else other than pork chops or chicken).
Other Taxi. Hydrofoil to Piraeus.

General
Ieraka (or Yeraka) is a gem of place that most people fall for on their first visit. The hamlet, a single line of houses sits wedged along the quay-front hemmed in by rocky slopes on either side. At the eastern end you look out to the cliffs blocking off the entrance and the western end opens up into a shallow lagoon. The locals are a friendly lot who now ease their winter

solitude with some summer income from the yachts that visit here.

On the northern entrance point are the ruins of ancient Ierakos or Ierax above the appropriately named Ak Kastro (Castle Cape). The ruins of the Mycenean acropolis are littered over the plateau above the cape. The inlet presumably served as the harbour for the ancient city.

Ak Ieraka

Nisis Dhaskalio

The sheer-sided "full-stop" of an islet in the large bay south of Ak Ierakas. In calm weather it is possible to anchor off in the bay although it is mostly fairly deep. There is also a cove to the south just north of Ak Kremmidhi where a yacht can anchor in calm weather. In either of these two bays there is a ground-swell if any swell at all is running outside.

Ormos Kremmidhi

The large bay just over a mile west of Ak Kremmidhi. In the approach care needs to be taken of a reef and shoal water off the coast just west of Ak Kremmidhi. The reef is deceptive and it is all too easy to cut the corner and shave it or worse. There are several anchorages around Ormos Kremmidhi.

1. On the east just inside the east entrance point. Subject to gusts off the land with the *meltemi*.

2. In the northeast although care is needed of a reef off the shore. Subject to gusts with the *meltemi* but good holding.

3. In the northwest corner. Also subject to gusts with the *meltemi* but probably the best place to be with the *meltemi* in the bay.

Ormos Palaio (Monemvasia)

The cove in the northwest corner of Kolpos Limiras. A tower on Ak Palaio Monemvasia is conspicuous and closer in the light structure on the east entrance point will be seen. Care needs to be taken of the reef running west from the east entrance point. Make your approach from the southwest.

Anchor in 6-10 metres on sand and weed, good holding. Care needs to be taken of large permanent moorings on the bottom further in from the 6 metre line. There are gusts into here with the *meltemi* but it affords the best shelter from a strong *meltemi* in Kolpos Limiras. Ashore there is a small fishing hamlet but no facilities. Around the bay to the west is a camping ground and the ruins of ancient Epidhavros-Limera established by colonists from the Epidhavros in the Argolid.

Monemvasia looking from the anchorage at Palaio Monemvasia.

N

5 ⚓

8

Ormos Kremmidhi

Gusts

Gusts

Gusts

10

10

10

10

6 Ak Kremmidhi

10

Palaia
Monemvasia

⚓

☼
Tr (conspic)
Fl.G.2·5s3M

Ormos Palaio

Beach

10

10

*Prevailing wind
when the meltemi
is not blowing*

(morning)

(afternoon)

(night)

10

10

Gusts

☼ Fl.5s6M

Monemvasia

Old village

See plan

0   1
Nautical Mile

Depths in Metres

MONEMVASIA AND APPROACHES

Monemvasia

The huge hump-backed headland is easily identified from the distance and once seen is unmistakable again.

Pilotage

Approach The high headland, looking like an island from the distance is conspicuous from some distance off. Closer in the houses of Yefira on the Peloponnese will be seen.

The light on the tip of Monemvasia

From the north the mole on the north side is easily identified. From the south the old village on the headland will be seen and the small fishing village.

Mooring **North Side.** Go stern or bows-to the inner half of the mole leaving the ferry and hydrofoil berths clear. Near the root of the mole a yacht should take care as the rocky bottom is uneven and ballasting extends a short distance off the quay. The bottom is mud and rocks, reasonable holding. Good protection from southerlies but with fresh to strong northeasterlies a surge builds up causing yachts to roll and snatch on lines ashore. Strong westerlies sometimes blow down off the hills onto the quay

South Side. Anchor off the fishing harbour in 6-12 metres on sand, rock and weed, mostly good holding. Good shelter from northerlies and southerlies do not usually blow home in the summer. However there is always some ground-swell here causing yachts to roll at anchor.

Note At the time of writing the new marina is under construction but is still some way off completion. The projected final form for the marina is given but there is no guarantee the actual finished marina will look like that shown. It will of course afford much improved shelter and facilities here.

Monemvasia lower town looking down from the summit. Nigel Patten.

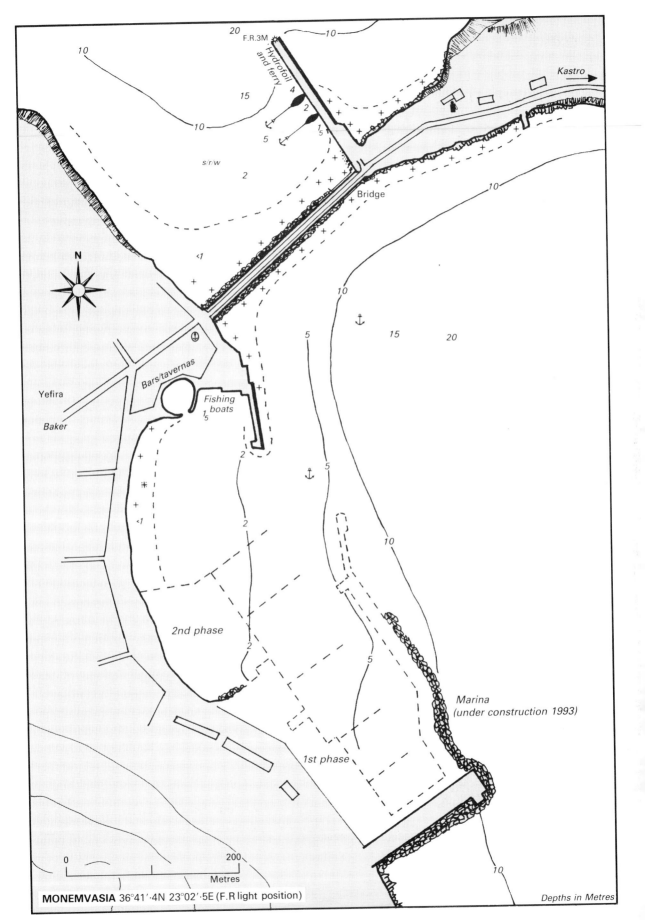

20 F.R.3M
10
Hydrofoil and ferry
Kastro →
10
15
4
2
10
s/r/w
5
1 5
2
Bridge
10
<1
10
N
10
5
15
20
Bars/tavernas
Fishing boats
1 5
5
2
<1
2
10
2nd phase
2
10
5
2
Marina (under construction 1993)
1st phase
10
0   200
Metres
MONEMVASIA 36°41'·4N 23°02'·5E (F.R light position)
Yefira
Baker
Depths in Metres

Facilities

Services Water delivered by tanker. Fuel delivered by mini-tanker or for small amounts go to the fuel station on the causeway.

Provisions Good shopping for all provisions in Yefira. Ice available.

Eating Out Numerous tavernas in the old town and in Yefira. The tavernas in the old town are inviting and the setting is romantic. In Yefira I favour one of the *ouzeries* on the edge of the fishing harbour which often have grilled octopus and good basic Greek fare. The *Pizzeria* at the root of the quay is also good value-bustling and friendly.

Other PO. OTE. Hire motorbikes and cars. *Malvasia Travel* in Yefira can usually sort out anything you want. Ferry and hydrofoil to Piraeus and points along the way.

General

The monolithic rock rising sheer out of the sea with the old village tucked onto the southern side is like an apparition, a chunk of the Middle Ages separated, as it is, by the causeway from the contemporary world. Monemvasia has been called the Gibraltar-of-the-east for obvious reasons but it is all the more impressive for being isolated from any rebuilding after the early 19th century and an historical preservation order should keep it that way. It is a "must" for anyone to see despite the inadequate shelter for yachts, at least until the new marina is finished.

The name Monemvasia means "single entrance" from the only access across what is now a causeway. The headland was once joined to the Peloponnese and Pausanias refers to it as Akra Minoa, Cape Minoa, suggesting there was

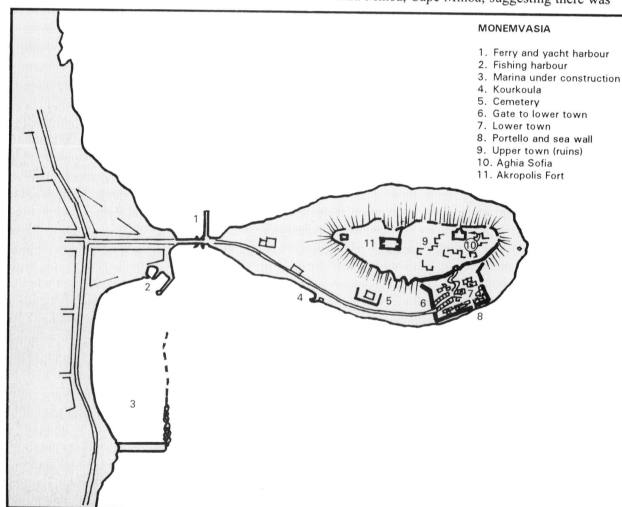

MONEMVASIA

1. Ferry and yacht harbour
2. Fishing harbour
3. Marina under construction
4. Kourkoula
5. Cemetery
6. Gate to lower town
7. Lower town
8. Portello and sea wall
9. Upper town (ruins)
10. Aghia Sofia
11. Akropolis Fort

Monemvasia in a 17th century engraving by Coronelli.

Monemvasia lower town looking from seaward.

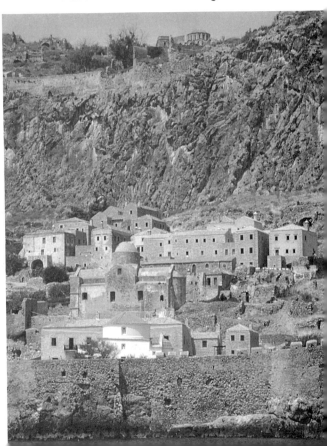

a Minoan colony here. In 375 AD a cataclysmic earthquake struck the region sinking many coastal cities beneath the sea and severing the headland from the coast and turning it into an island. It was intermittently settled after this, but it was not until the 6th century that the Byzantines built a substantial town on the summit and fortified it with thick walls.

The lower town on the slopes wasn't built until some 400 years later when Monemvasia had become an important trading post for the Byzantines. From the fortified rock they could control the gateway to the Aegean around Cape Malea and their various settlements on the Peloponnese. It was briefly taken by the Franks under Villehardouin in 1249 but the Byzantines soon got it back in 1263 and were to hold it for another 130 years.

By now the Turkish threat was looming over the horizon from the east and the city looked to the Venetians for security. Not surprisingly the

Venetians snapped the offer up and added Monemvasia to their already impressive list of fortresses around the Peloponnese protecting the trade route from Asia Minor. The Turks bided their time and in 1540 took the city only to have the Venetians come back under Morosini and retake it in 1690. It couldn't last and in 1715 the Turks were back again to stay until the Greek War of Independence in 1821.

Monemvasia was well known around the world, as Malvoisie to the Franks and Malmsey to the English, for the sweet red wine which was shipped from here but probably not produced here as is sometimes inferred. It is interesting that a heavy sweet wine will travel better than lighter more delicate wines and Malmsey was much in demand for the long voyages of the time.

All these sieges and counter-sieges account for much of the continuous strengthening of the fortifications on the island. Everybody was at it. The Venetians beefed up the Byzantine walls and the Turks in turn added more walls and towers. The old town at the top was originally reached via a path from the causeway leading up to a huge gate, but in the 15th century the Turks closed it off with a thick wall leaving the only access via the lower town. As you walk up the narrow winding path to what became the main gateway to the old town it is not difficult to imagine what it was like for attackers told to get on up there and engage the enemy. To me the path up to the top with thick walls and hedged in with banked corners looks suspiciously like a giant pin-ball alley that a giant rock pin-ball released from the top would

Monemvasia. Looking down to the lower town from the steep path leading up to the summit.

rattle down at increasing speed squashing any human flesh foolish enough to be in its way.

On the summit of the rock there is little left of the buildings of the old town save the defensive walls and the Byzantine church of Aghia Sofia. It sits precariously on the edge of the northern cliffs, as if perched on the air, with a view out over the sea and coast that is giddying and not one for those who suffer from vertigo, especially if any wind is tugging at your clothes.

Down below the lower town has been largely preserved and reconstructed. Many of the older houses are Byzantine with 16th and 17th century additions while there are 18th and 19th century houses and adornments as well. The whole mixture of Byzantine, Venetian and Turkish with a bit of neo-classical thrown in is bordered by defensive walls with streets that were designed for donkeys and handcarts rather than motor vehicles- which mercifully are not allowed past the main gate into the town. Many of the houses have been converted into tavernas, bars, souvenir shops and boutiques which if sometimes a little precious, at least do not intrude on the character of the place. The stones of the main street are now worn smooth with the tramping of thousands of feet in the summer and "grippy" shoes rather than deck shoes should be worn.

The island was originally joined to the coast by a wooden bridge which the Venetians replaced with an elegant stone bridge. It had fourteen arches with a central wooden section which could be removed to prevent access in a siege. Bits of the bridge remain under the causeway now connecting the island to the mainland. The settlement of Yefira (the name means "bridge") on the Peloponnese coast is now the main settlement where most of the population lives.

Ay Fokas

A cove and small fishing harbour 5½ miles south of Monemvasia. I have never actually put in here as the wind and swell have always been a little too much for rock-hopping, but in calm weather it could be worth exploring.

Ak Maleas

The great rocky cape that a yacht must round before proceeding up into Lakonikos Kolpos. It is a stark place, forbidding, and worthy of the saying Strabo said was uttered by Greek sailors as they rounded it to head westwards: Formidatum Malea caput-"Double Cape Malea and forget your native home"

From the north the first thing you will see is the lighthouse perched on a splintered outcrop before the cape proper. Once around the cape a hermitage with several sun-white dwellings and a church are like a saving signal from the confused swell always encountered here. When Alphonse de Lamartine rounded the cape in the middle of the 19th century he left this bleak account of the hermit on the cape.

"We doubled the cape so closely that we could distinguish his long white beard, his staff, his chaplet, his hood of brown felt, like that of sailors in winter. He went on his knees as we passed, with his face turned towards the sea, as if he were imploring the succour of Heaven for the unknown strangers on this perilous passage. The wind, which issues furiously from the mountain-gorges of Laconia, as soon as you double the rock of the cape, began to resound in our sails, and make the two vessels roll and stagger, covering the sea with foam as far as the eye could reach. A new sea was opening before us. The hermit, in order to follow us still farther with his eyes, ascended the crest of a rock, and we distinguished him there, on his knees, and motionless, as long as we were in sight of the cape."

A. de Lamartine. *Travels in the East* 1850

The hermitage on Ak Maleas.

Passage on to Kithera and Lakonikos Kolpos

From Ak Maleas most yachts will head for either Ay'Nikolaos or Kapsali on Kithera or for Nisos Elafonisos or Porto Kayio. Care is needed in Stenon Elafonisos, the channel between Ak Maleas and Kithera, of the large amount of commercial shipping passing through the strait. There will always be one or two ships around at the very least.

Passage to Kithera is straightforward, the island can be seen from Maleas, though care is needed in the lee of the island where there can be strong gusts with the prevailing westerlies. Passage to Elafonisos is also straightforward although there can be strong gusts into Ormos Vatika and off Elafonisos with a strong *meltemi*.

There is nearly always a south-going current from Ak Kamili to Maleas, often as much as 1½-2 knots which makes going south great but plugging up to the north from the cape a tedious affair. The current also causes a confused swell around the cape with current lines and little overfalls which can become a problem with strong southerlies. The cape has a reputation for bad weather and it can be a dangerous place, but do not be put off by Alphonse de Lamartine's description as in the summer you can often get around in a near calm with luck and no depressions around.

Appendix

APPENDIX 1

Common Greek terms and abbreviations used in the text and plans

Akra (Ak)	Cape
Andi (Anti)	Opposite
Ayios (Ay)	Saint
Dhiavlos	Strait or channel
Dhiorix	Channel or canal
Dhromos	Roadstead
Faros	Lighthouse
Ifalos (If or I)	Reef
Isthmos	Isthmus
Kavos	Cape
Khersonisos	Headland
Kolpos	Gulf
Limin (L)	Harbour
Molos	Breakwater or mole
Moni	Monastery
Nisaki	Islet
Nisos/Nisi/Nisia (N)	Island(s)
Notios	Southern
Ormos (O)	Bay
Ormiskos	Cove
Oros	Mountain
Pelagos	Sea
Pirgos	Tower
Porto	Small harbour
Potamos (Pot)	River
Pounda	Cape or point
Stenon	Strait
Thalassa	Sea
Vorios	Northern
Vrakhonisis	Rocky islet
Vrakhos	Rock

APPENDIX 2

A few useful words in Greek

General

yes	ne
no	okhi
please	parakalo
thank you	efharisto
OK	endaksi
hot	zeste
cold	krio
here	etho
there	eki
hello	herete
goodbye	adio
good morning	kalamera
good evening	kalaspera
good night	kalanikta
good	kalo
bad	kako
today	simera
tomorrow	avrio
later	meta
now	tora
I want	ego thelo
where is	pou inai
big	megalo
small	mikro
one	ena
two	thio
three	tria
four	teissera
five	pende
six	hexa
seven	hepta
eight	octo
nine	enai
ten	theca

Shopping

apples	mila
apricots	verikoka
aubergines	melitzana
baker	fourno
beans	fassolia
beef	mouskhari
biscuits	biscottes
bread	psomi
butcher	hassapiko
butter	voutiro

carrots	carotta
cheese	tiri
chicken	kotopoulo
chocolate	socolata
coffee	kavé
cucumber	angouri
eggs	avga
fish shop	psaroplion
flour	alevri
garlic	scordo
green pepper	piperi
grocer	bakaliko
ham	zambon
honey	meli
jam	marmelada
lamb	arinaki
lemon	limoni
margarine	margarini
meat	kreas
melon (water-)	karpouzi
milk	gala
mutton	arni
oil	lathi
onions	kremidia
oranges	portokalia
parsley	maidano
peach	rodakina
pepper	piperi
pork	khirino
potatoes	patatas
rice	rizi
salt	alati
sugar	zahari
tea	tsai
tomatoes	dhomates
water	nero
wine	krassi
yoghurt	yaourti

APPENDIX 3

Useful Books

Admiralty Publications

Mediterranean Pilot Vol IV Covers the Aegean.
List of Lights Vol E Covers the Mediterranean, Black and Red Seas.

Yachtsman's Pilots

Greek Waters Pilot Rod Heikell Imray. Covers all Greek waters in a single volume.
Aegean H M Denham. Covers the whole Aegean. Classic guide though no longer revised and kept up to date.

Other Guides

Blue Guide to Greece Edited by Stuart Rossiter A & C Black.
Berlitz Guide to Athens Berlitz. Good compact guide.
The Saronic John Fawssett Roger Lascelles.
The Greek Islands Lawrence Durrell Faber. Good photos and eloquent prose.
The Greek Islands Ernle Bradford. Collins Companion Guide.
The Rough Guide to Greece Ellingham, Jansz and Fisher. RKP. Down to earth guide.
The Colossus of Maroussi Henry Miller. Penguin. Arguably his best piece of writing, fiction included.
Fortresses and Castles of Greek Islands and *Fortresses and Castles of Greece* Vol II Alexander Paradissis Efstathiados Group. Detailed guides available in Greece.
The Venetian Empire Jan Morris Penguin. Readable account of the Venetian maritime empire.

General

A Literary Companion to Travel in Greece Edited by Richard Stoneman Penguin.
The Ulysses Voyage Tim Severin Hutchinson
The Hill of Kronos Peter Levi. Zenith.
Hellas Nicholas Gage Collins Harvill

Flora and Fauna

Flowers of Greece and the Aegean Anthony Huxley and William Taylor
Flowers of the Mediterranean Anthony Huxley and Oleg Polunin. Both the above have excellent colour photos and line drawings for identification.
Trees and Bushes of Britain and Europe Oleg Polunin Paladin.
The Hamlyn Guide to Birds of Britain and Europe Bruun, Delin and Svensson Hamlyn.
The Hamlyn Guide to the Flora and Fauna of the Mediterranean A C Campbell Hamlyn Good guide to marine life.

Food

Greek Cooking Robin Howe
Food of Greece Vilma Chantiles
The Best of Greek Cooking Chrissa Paradissis

APPENDIX 4

Beaufort Wind Scale

B'fort No.	Wind Descrip	Effect on sea	Effect on land	Wind Speed knots mph	Wave Height (metres)
0	Calm	Like a mirror	Smoke rises vertically	less than 1	
1	Light	Ripples, no foam	Direction shown by smoke	1-3 1-3	-
2	Light breeze	Small wavelets, crests do not break	Wind felt on face, leaves rustle	4-6 4-7	0.2-0.3
3	Gentle breeze	Large wavelets, some white horses	Wind extends light flag	7-10 8-12	0.6-1.0
4	Moderate breeze	Small waves, frequent white horses	Small branches move dust raised	1-16 13-18	1.0-1.5
5	Fresh breeze	Moderate waves, some spray	Small trees sway	17-21 19-24	1.8-2.5
6	Strong breeze	Large waves form, white crests, some spray	Large branches move	22-27 25-31	3.0-4.0
7	Near gale	Sea heaps up, white foam, waves begin to streak	Difficult to walk in wind	28-33 32-38	4.0-6.0
8	Gale	Moderately high waves	Twigs break off trees, walking impeded	34-40 39-46	5.5-7.5
9	Strong gale	High waves, dense foam, wave crests break, heavy spray	Slates blow off roofs	41-47 47-54	7.0-9.75
10	Storm	Very high waves, sea appears white, visibility affected	Trees uprooted, structural damage	48-56 66-63	9.0-12.5
11	Violent storm	Exceptionally high waves, wave crests blown off, badly impaired	Widespread damage	57-65 64-75	11.3-16
12	Hurricane	Winds of this force seldom encountered for any duration in the Mediterranean.			

APPENDIX 5

Useful conversions

1 inch = 2.54 centimetres (roughly 4in = 10cm)
1 centimetre = 0.394 inches

1 foot = 0.305 metres (roughly 3ft = 10 metres)
1 metre = 3.281 feet

1 pound = 0.454 kilograms (roughly 10lbs = 4.5 kgms)
1 kilogram = 2.205 pounds

1 mile = 1.609 kilometres (roughly 10 miles = 16 km)
1 kilometre = 0.621 miles

1 nautical mile = 1.1515 miles
1 mile = 0.8684 nautical miles

1 acre = 0.405 hectares (roughly 10 acres = 4 hectares)
1 hectare = 2.471 acres

1 gallon = 4.546 litres (roughly 1 gallon = 4.5 litres)
1 litre = 0.220 gallons

Temperature scale

$t°F$ to $t°C$ is $5/9 (t°F - 32) = t°C$

$t°C$ to $t°F$ is $9/5 (t°C + 32) = t°F$

So
70°F = 21.1°C		20°C = 68°F
80°F = 26.7°C		30°C = 86°F
90°F = 32.2°C		40°C = 104°F

Index

Imray

PILOT BOOKS

The following are available:

Greek Waters Pilot

Rod Heikell

The definitive pilot for the area, covering the Ionian and Aegean and is the recognised companion for cruising in Greece.

Italian Waters Pilot

Rod Heikell

Covers the western and southern coasts of Italy from the Riviera to Brindisi and includes Sardinia and Sicily.

Adriatic Pilot

T & D Thompson

Covers eastern Italy, Slovenia, Croatia and Albania

Turkish Waters and Cyprus Pilot

Rod Heikell

Covers the Aegean and Mediterranean coast of Turkey from Istanbul to Syria. Cyprus is included in this volume. In the same style as *Greek Waters Pilot*, this is the only comprehensive guide to the area. It has been completely updated and now includes the Turkish Black Sea coast.

RCC Pilotage Foundation

North Africa

Hans van Rijn

Covers the coastlines of Morocco, Algeria and Tunisia from Tangier and Gibraltar to Lampedusa and Malta. Fully illustrated with detailed plan and colour photographs.

Mediterranean Cruising Handbook

Rod Heikell

A general compendium of information for anyone planning to cruise in the Mediterranean. This work is also a useful cockpit reference and is packed with essential information on each country in the Mediterranean.

Full details of all these and other publications are available from the Publishers.

Imray, Laurie, Norie & Wilson Ltd

Wych House, The Broadway, St Ives, Huntingdon, Cambs. PE17 4BT England
Tel (0480) 462114 *Fax* (0480) 496109

Also available for the Ionian and Aegean

IMRAY TETRA Charts for the Mediterranean Ionian and Aegean

The chart size is 640 x 900mm. The sheets are available flat or folded and printed on waterproof material.

G1 Mainland Greece and the Peloponnese 1:729,000
G11 North Ionian Islands 1:182,400
G12 South Ionian Islands 1:188,200
G13 Gulfs of Patras and Corinth 1:218,900
G14 Saronic and Argolic Gulf 1:189,000
G2 Aegean Sea (North Part) 1:748,000
G25 Northern Sporades and North Nisos Evvoia 1:186,800
G3 Aegean Sea (South Part) 1:758,000
G31 Northern Cyclades 1:189,700
G32 Southern Sporades and Coast of Turkey 1:189,700
G33 Southern Cyclades (*Sheet 1 – West*) 1:190,0
G34 Southern Cyclades (*Sheet 2 – East*) 1:190,0

These publications are also available in the Ionian from Contract Yacht Services, Petrou Filippa 3a, Levkas 31 1 and in Athens from Pelagos Marine SA, 19 Poseidonos Kalamaki 17455 Athens.

IMRAY FOR BRITISH ADMIRALTY CHARTS

Imrays are main stockholding agents for Hydrographic office publications. We hold a complete inventory of charts and associated publications, lights and radio lists for the Eastern Mediterranean.

Charts can be posted anywhere in the world and discounts are available to trade customers.

Write, telephone or *fax* for a complete catalogue.

at name_____

ipper_____

ew list

ate	Time	Wind	Sea	Course °T	Compass Course	Distance	Speed	Current	Remarks, events, position fixes

Fuel_____Hrs Date/time_____

Water_____Hrs Date/time_____

Motor hours_____hours

Log total_____nautical miles

Boat name_____

Skipper_____

Crew list

Date	Time	Wind	Sea	Course °T	Compass Course	Distance	Speed	Current	Remarks, events, position fixe

Fuel_____Hrs Date/time_____

Water_____Hrs Date/time_____

Motor hours_____hours

Log total_____nautical miles

at name_____

ipper_____

ew list

te	Time	Wind	Sea	Course °T	Compass Course	Distance	Speed	Current	Remarks, events, position fixes

el_____Hrs Date/time_____

iter_____Hrs Date/time_____

tor hours_____hours

g total_____nautical miles

oat name_____

kipper_____

rew list

ate	Time	Wind	Sea	Course °T	Compass Course	Distance	Speed	Current	Remarks, events, position fixes

el_____Hrs Date/time_____

ter_____Hrs Date/time_____

tor hours_____hours

g total_____nautical miles

SARONIC
192 pp
Crown Metric Quarto
246mm x 189mm